Aw[illegible]me Animals & Purrfect Pets

Edited by Jonathan Fisher

First published in Great Britain in 2011 by:

Young Writers
Remus House
Coltsfoot Drive
Peterborough
PE2 9BF
Telephone: 01733 890066
Website: www.youngwriters.co.uk

Book Design by Ali Smith & Tim Christian

SB ISBN 978-0-85739-253-4

Foreword

Awesome Animals & Purrfect Pets is a collection resulting from one of our most popular themes here at Young Writers - poetry inspired by pets and the animal kingdom.

Within these pages young poets tell us why creatures great and small are so important to them and they share with us the many tall tales involving their beloved pets. Whether their best friends are furry or feathered, scaly or slimy, they are considered one of the family and are loved and adored by the poets in this anthology.

As always, the selection process was a very enjoyable experience, as the contributors share their heartfelt feelings in verse: sometimes comedic, sometimes in remembrance, and often with accompanying photos to make their words come to life.

After flicking through this rewarding collection, we're sure you'll agree - wouldn't life be quiet and boring without animals to brighten up our days!

Contents

The Poems

Cookie - My Guinea Pig!

He's a full time eater,
He bounds around his cage,
He's a nice hand heater,
His coat is white and beige.

His eyes are black and beady,
His ears - small and pink.
He is forever greedy,
He's growing up, I think.

He's a water drinker,
His energy never runs out!
A sly and clever thinker,
Of that I do not doubt!

Cookie's not that lazy;
He's still a playful tot,
Even though he's crazy,
I love him such a lot!

Rebecca Emma Guy (11)

Winner

Congratulations, Rebecca. Your great poem has won you a fantastic animal adoption pack for a year.

Well done!

My Pet

I love my pet
He is the best
He is better than all the rest.
I love my pet
He's my buddy
He likes to get very muddy.
I love my pet
He's fat and pink
Oh my goodness he can stink.
I love my pet
He squeaks and squeals
He loves his food and his meals.
I love my pet
He's very big
Yes you've guessed, he is a pig!

Megan Ellison (9)

The Trade Of The Leopard

Her eyes shone like headlights in the dark,
Her radiant fur of intricate patterns gleamed in the light of the moon.
The tracker, the stalker, the hunter,
Hidden in the long grass, ready to pounce,
Crouched, watching the prey's every move,
Silently, patiently, waiting,
Silent, watchful, remaining,
Then she powerfully leaps into the air,
Using her mighty hindquarters,
She runs; the prey flees.
Running, fast, concentrated,
On and on, until,
She sinks her colossal paws into the prey's back,
She has done it,
Mother, provider, leopard,
This is her trade.

Kate Amelia Sibbald (10)

The Seal

I am a seal, I am shiny and smooth
I am flippy and floppy
That's how I move
I swim in the ocean
It's large and it's wide
Catching the fish brought in on the tide
I have many friends who now live in a zoo
But I prefer freedom,
Wouldn't you?

Hannah Warham (9)

My Pet Rabbit

If rabbits were like kangaroos,
They would jump up right in front of you.
It is like a cuddly bear
That will hug you everywhere.
It will hug you when you eat,
When you sleep, when you cheat,
And when you creep.

It will eat carrots every day
Just like you as you say
Give it a carrot
Just for a marrot
And that is what you say.

Aisha Patel (9)

My Pet Budgies

If my pet budgies were like parrots
They would chirp all day,
And get on my nerves.

They both live in a lovely white cage
And play beautifully together.

With beautiful colours
And soft wings,
They are just the right size for me
But have silky smooth skin.

I love my birds
They are the best.

Farrah Asif (10)

My Dog, Skip

If a labrador was as golden as sand
It would jump up and lick your face
Some say they are cute and furry
Or some say are big and hairy
I say my dog is my best friend and
I love him very much.

Joshua Michael Shaun Daly (9)

My Pets

I have a greyhound,
Named Ebony.
She has a soft brindle coat
That is as soft as silk
She is very cute.

Flake the guinea pig
Is owned by me
With brown and caramel fur
She is so very cute,
She likes a cuddle.

Rebecca Clarke (9)

My Animal

He sits, he waits, he sneers, he . . .
Chases
He catches, he wins, he kills, he . . .
Goes

He is the one that I look up to,
Fast and furious, yet clever and smart.
He is the one that I'm proud of,
You watch him and anxiety fills your heart.

Others are scared of him,
But I have no fear.
The harm is only there if you make it,
It's better if you stand clear.

I will walk up to him,
For I am no threat
I can read his mind,
He knows who I am
I talk his language
Yet he doesn't talk mine.

He is a cheetah and I am just . . .
Me
We are so different but so alike.

Siriluck Sara Collins (13)

Glen And Austin

G len is my nine-year-old dog,
L oving and caring he is.
E xcited to see me every day,
N ever too far away.

A ustin is my puppy, he is one year old,
U nder my feet all the time,
S illy and sweet,
T error he can be,
I nquisitive and nosy,
N aughty but nice.

Samantha Gemmell (9)

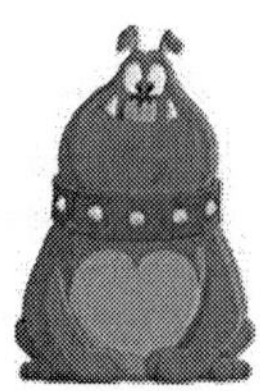

My Dream Iguana

I dream of him in scaly skin,
Although I know he's very thin
Deep blue eyes,
It's easy for him to compromise,
He swims so gently,
He's smooth like an American Bentley,
These are the qualities my dream Iguana has.

Jasmine Gurung (11)

George, The Dog

George, the dog, oh George, the dog
Is adorable by name and nature.
He sits in the shimmering perfectly-made basket,
But is certainly no diminutive traitor.

He could eat a horse but I do say of course
He does not eat his greens!

Why he could eat practically anything
Except those horrible peppers.
'Please don't make me eat them,
I'd rather eat a letter!'

He's an extremely rapid Jack Russell
(Who would hate it if he didn't have big muscles).
The avarice dog is very flexible
But when it comes to the evening
He just sleeps on the floor
(Which he likes best of all).

His bark is so clamorous,
It can reach up to one hundred decibels
But George is still extremely amorous.

He is very vigilant and adventurous,
He is also extremely cool
But although he has a loud bark
He is never, oh never belligerent.

William Freeman (10)

What Am I?

Bubbles floating from my mouth,
Swimming round and round,
My tail big and wavy,
Not making one sound,
My eyes are big and boggley,
And my fins go flick and swish,
Have you guessed what I am yet?
I'm a fish!

Kirsten Jessica Bath (10)

Perro

P is for playful, he is very playful
E is for enjoying, he is enjoying himself
R is for rolling, he is rolling around
R is for rabbit, he has a friend rabbit called Thumper
O is for over, he runs over the hill.

Caitlin Hine (9)

Pippin

My dog's name is Pippin,
He gives you a good licking!
And his big black paws . . .
Sometimes scratch at the doors!
His big black button nose,
Will sniff you from head to toe.
He's a big strong boy,
Which gives him joy!
When the girl dogs see him on the street,
Their hearts skip a beat!
He still is very alive,
Although he's nearly five!
He is a puppy at heart,
Oh, and beans make him fart!

Charlotte Turner (12)

Barking Mad

I go barking mad for dogs;
Jack Russells and Staffs;
I love the way they beg and roll,
We all have lots of laughs.

They catch a ball, we chuck;
They chase a stick, we throw;
We tickle their bellies gently,
They're great, don't you think so.

I love their buggy eyes,
I love their runs and jogs;
So all that I can say is,
    I love dogs!

Steffan Rhys Taylor (11)

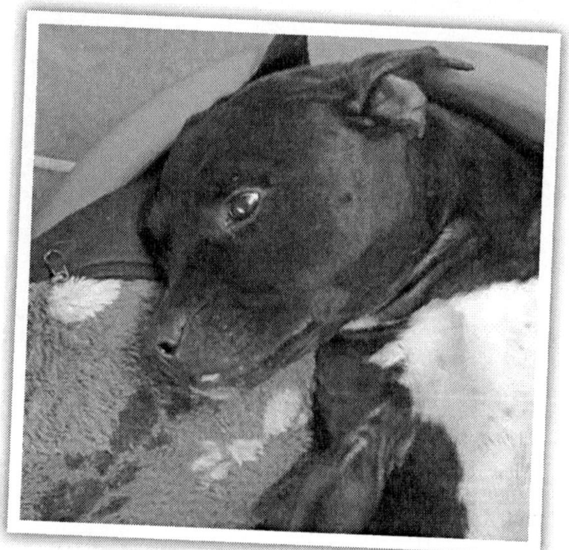

Mice

One day in the house,
Out ran a little mouse.

Stopped quickly by the cat,
And then eaten on the mat.

Inside the cat's big belly,
It was filled with orange jelly.

The mouse had a thought,
He tickled the cat like he'd been taught.

The cat spewed out the poor little mouse,
Who ran and ran back into the house.

Euan Pringle (9)

This Is The Paw

This is the paw that I cleaned when dirty,
That then got muddy and I cleaned again.

This is the paw that caught the ball,
That got dropped down and caught again.

This is the paw that scratched the door,
That go painted over and scratched again.

This is the paw that bopped the cat,
Who bopped me back . . . Ouch!

Liam Jones (10)

My Shih-Tzu Suzey And Her Bath

With her head held high
And her bum tucked in
She ran as fast as a bullet
Although she's quite thin!
The bath makes her crazy!

Her face covered in suds
With doggy aroma in the air
She barks and she whimpers
Until she jumps out without a moment to spare!
The bath makes her crazy!

When cuddled in a towel
She does look rather like a floozy
But she's cute and cuddly and I love her,
Because she's my Suzey!

Anna Stainton (13)

Racing Stripes

Stripes the zebra loves to race,
But zebras aren't supposed to race,
That's Stripes' case.

He likes to run round and round,
And would love to be watched by a large crowd,
That would make Stripes proud.

Then came the big race,
So Stripes had better up his pace,
Cross the finish line the race is up,
Stripes the zebra is number one.

Charlotte Bird (12)

A Poem About Giraffes

My favourite animal is the giraffe,
I wonder how they take a bath?
I love their skin with their crazy dots
They look a bit like leopard spots.
I love their long, handsome necks,
From so high up we must look like specks!
I love the way they move so gracefully,
If animals had fashion, they'd dress so tastefully.
But most of all I love them so
'Cause they're so high and other animals are all down low.

Lewis Low (10)

Funny Bunny

P ickle is a funny bunny
I like to watch him run through his tunnel
C uddles we like to share
K ate and Mark are his owners and my auntie and uncle
L ove each other and tickles together
E very day and for ever, Pickle is my best friend.

Tamar Redwood (6)

Animal - Haikus

Monkey
Leaping through the air
Chasing through the undergrowth
Eating bananas.

Lion
Chasing after prey
Stalking, silent, through grasslands
Cute cubs play fighting.

Penguin
Swimming under ice
Penguins waddle together
Catching fish for tea.

Eleanor De Boise (9)

A Poem About My Dog

His name is Eddie,
He's not very steady.
I love him a lot,
He's the best dog I've got.
Digging earth with his paws,
Chewing bones with his jaws.
His licky tongue is nice and wet,
I hope he never goes to the vet.
I love him so much, he's cute and sweet,
His heart is so big, I can hear it beat!

Ross Low (7)

Untitled

Slippery snakes and slimy snails,
Meet clean wagging dogs' tails,
Purring cats and dark haired bats,
Meet cockroaches under mats.

Snapping jaws and padded paws,
Meet animals from the great outdoors,
Monkeys, apes and orang-utans,
Meet animals from foreign lands.

From frogs, birds and big bears,
Come lots and lots of animal pairs.

Raiyanne Emily Mohammed-Brown (12)

Molly

Molly is the cutest of kittens.
A ginger tabby,
White paws like mittens.

My sister, Isobel treats her like a 'babby',
And pushes her round in her doll's pram;
Much to Molly's disgust.
My sister thinks that she's her mam.
Molly looks, and is gone with a whoosh and a gust.

Finlay Holborn (9)

The Stalker

Every day I see her face,
Running down like it's a race,
Looking through the patio door,
Licking the puddle from the floor.

Nobody really knows her name,
But we all know why she came,
The stalker cat is what I call her,
Find that's the name which I prefer.

Did I tell you she's a cat?
Her face looks like a little brown bat,
Big blue eyes and light brown fur,
When I stroke her she goes 'purr'!

The other cat she follows a lot,
Especially when the weather's hot,
Ready to pounce when the time is right,
Giving the other cat a great big fright.

I love these cats so much, it's true,
If you had them you'd feel the same too.

Samantha Gower (13)

Billy, The Toy Poodle Puppy

Billy is my poodle,
He's as thin as a noodle.
His fur is snowy,
His black eyes all glowy.
Billy, my toy poodle.

The best friend of Billy
Is a dog called Milly.
They play in the park
Until it gets dark.
Billy, my toy poodle.

When we come home,
He grabs his comb
And gets lots of fuss and attention.

Billy is the greatest of all,
He chases his tail and also his ball.
He's my perfect pet,
Billy, my toy poodle.

Grace Sinden (14)

All About Animals And Pets

All sorts of animals are around you today
Some are even many miles away
There are wild animals
(And lots are mammals)
There are lions with their beautiful manes
And elephants with their trunks like chains
Then there's perfect pets
They run faster than jets
With lovely dogs that run fast
And hamsters that never come last
Hopefully that shows animals are best
And they will always beat the rest.

Alice Daniel (9)

Misty

I have a little kitten, Misty is her name,
Life to Misty, well, I think it's just a game.
She has black fluffy fur, the colour of midnight,
And when she plays with her little string ball, it really is a sight.

Misty's eyes are the brightest emerald green,
I have to admit she is the cutest cat I've seen.
Whenever I pour her a saucer of milk she always dashes there,
When she drinks I stroke her soft fur, but I know she doesn't care.

Misty then plays with her little string ball
Rolling around her body so petite so small.
Then her ears pricked, Misty jumps to her feet,
Pads over to the fire, embracing the heat.

Misty then shuts her eyes, into the land of dreams,
Dreams of happiness, or so it seems.
I then cuddle Misty, hold her very tight,
Dreaming together through the long, dark night.

Charlotte Isabella Hill (13)

All Cats - Haiku

We all care for cats
We love them and they love us
Cats are beautiful!

Khadija Begum (10)

My Useless Dog

I have a dog
His name is Fred.
He won't fetch,
He won't play dead.

I have a dog
His name is Fred.
I want to play with him
But he's asleep on my bed.

I have a dog
His name is Fred.
His favourite colours are
Blue and red.

Gurmanik Singh (9)

My Panda's Whizzing World

I adopted a panda called Zhu Xiong
When I went to see it, it started singing a song.
It eats bamboo and drinks shampoo
What on earth does that panda get up to?
The week after that it made friends with a cat
Then a rat then a bat.
How could my panda do that?
The next time I went to see it
I got hit, it was playing cricket!
That's what my panda gets up to.

Alice Mitchell (9)

Mollie

Mollie is a poodle; her coat is black as coal.
Given a chance she will nibble your clothes until she makes a hole!
At fourteen years she is getting on but doesn't seem to care,
She chases round the garden pretending she's a hare.
When walking her each evening it really makes her smile.
She could run for England at twenty to the mile.
She's not a pretty looking dog and her bottom jaw sticks out
But her owner Elise still loves her, of that there is no doubt.

Elise Talbot (10)

I Love Animals

I love animals everywhere
In the sea, sky and in the air.
Some go squawk and others neigh, bark and call,
I even like the ones that say nothing at all.
There are lots of animals in the whole wide world
But alas my favourite is the humming bird.
It flies over London's rooftops
And at night when most of the world stops.
I love animals everywhere
But not everyone cares.

Maria McSweeney (12)

Puppies And Dogs

Cute little pup
Running around,
I wish she would go on the ground
Instead of jumping up and down!

Dogs may be big,
Dogs may be small,
Dogs aren't giraffes,
They're not that tall!

Puppies grow into dogs,
Dogs get stronger,
These animals like playing,
Their days get longer!

Holly Cobb (7)

My Amazing Dog, Rocco

My amazing dog can run faster than a cheetah
He eats and eats until he explodes

My amazing dog, Rocco
Always takes me around
He is always begging,
More and more until he gets some food.

My amazing dog, Rocco
Is the best dog ever!

Kai Gough (8)

My Pet Cat

My pet cat is called Alec,
He is black and white and is eight years old.
He is a good hunter.
Sadly, he catches little birds,
Rats and mice for his prey.
He munches them up like a biscuit.
He is very kind to young little me.
Alec likes swinging toys and string to play with.
He likes his tummy being tickled
But hates being picked up.
He is like a kitten on the bed when he sleeps.
I love my Alec cat.

Katerina Sadry-Cade (7)

The Magic Of The Heart Of A Button

The dark, chocolate-brown eyes gazing at you
The neighing of excitement leads to the swift mane
Shadowed by long glowing hair shining
The horseshoes clip-clopping down the village road
It brings the music into your soul
The horseshoe of the heart
The magic of friendliness
He gives the attention to his foal Cocoa
The way he chases rabbits and butterflies in those lime fields
Button is a lovely golden horse
Like all the other animals was created for a reason
To bring joy into our lives
Which will go on for generations.

Leony Shannon Hill (12)

Different Animals!

You look into the world,
See lots of animals,
Like a monkey named Milly,
A penguin named Polly,
And lots more.

You look into the world,
See lots of animals,
Like a donkey named Dilly,
Roger the rabbit,
And lots more.

You look into the world
And see . . .
Awesome animals
And . . .
Purrfect pets!

Merilliss Elysee (10)

My Dog

My dog can jump through a hoop.
He is very, very good
And can be very, very kind to you.
He can eat a bone
And by the next day it will be gone.
And that is all my dog can do.
Yes that is all my dog can do.

Rebekah Paterson (6)

My Cat, Daisy

I have a cat called Daisy,
She can sometimes be a little lazy.
Sometimes even crazy,
This is my cat, Daisy.

She eats a lot of food
And often can be in a mood.
She even sticks out her tongue,
Which I find very rude.
This is my cat, Daisy.

Daisy hates being taken to the vet,
She hates the smell I bet.
She dislikes getting wet,
But Daisy is the paw-fect pet!

Nicky Jeffs (12)

My Pet Dinosaur

I have a pet dinosaur,
Which proves a little messy,
But Reggie my dino,
Is always very friendly.

He's a happy-go-lucky guy,
Never moody or upset,
And he loves to take baths,
Jump in puddles and get wet.

He adores it when it rains,
And takes baths in the pond,
Splishing and sploshing,
Of tidal waves he is fond.

He loves chocolate and cookies,
And piles of whipped cream,
Just like any normal kid,
As scary as he may seem.

But he's terrified of thunder,
And he hides inside the shed,
He can do lots of tricks,
Including playing dead.

If I'm late and miss the school bus,
Reggie has a special job,
I ride to school on his back,
It's really not a prob.

But I have a little problem,
Not one person believes me,
They all have a laugh at Reggie,
Cos they think he's imaginary.

Lauren Rebecca Flynn (12)

The Lonely Tiger

It was a wonderful day
So I went out to play
After we went to the zoo
We saw giraffes and
Other animals too
I looked around then I gazed
I was so amazed
I saw a tiger
But it was a lonely tiger
Why was he lonely
I felt sad and even quite mad
That the lonely tiger seemed sad
Why was he lonely
He never had a honey
So I called out and said,
'God loves you, now go to bed,'
He looked and smiled
To me the child
I felt so happy
He was not lonely
Anymore . . .
But then something struck me
Mum isn't it time for tea?

Eskarda Sundein Matthew-Shaw (9)

Skitty Kitty

Skitty Kitty Jasmine Puss
She'll always come to you for fuss
She'll pout about all sweet and cute
She'll chase your hands around in loops
Going strong, all soft and fluffy,
She'll cheer you up when you feel huffy
Goodbye for now, we'll see you soon
Our cute, adorable, feline buffoon.

Crysania Conyers (12)

My Dog, Daisy

My dog, Daisy, sleeps all the time
Only wakes up at dinnertime
It doesn't matter how young or old
Keeps on doing as she's told
Well done Daisy
Well done dog
She's good but still can't jog,
On her bed, sleeps like a log
She never barks
She never bathes
My dog, Daisy
She's very lazy.

Noah Fitzgerald (12)

Chubby Gubby

I have a pet goldfish called Gubby
He's round and remarkably chubby
He swims round and round without making a sound
My lovely goldfish, Gubby.

He glides through his castle
Without any hassle
My lovely goldfish, Gubby.

When his fins wiggle
He makes me giggle
My lovely goldfish, Gubby.

He's as fast as a lightning bolt
He never comes to a halt
My lovely goldfish, Gubby.

He's my best pet yet
Never needed the vet
Oh how I love my Gubby!

Erin Elizabeth Collins (9)

Button

Cute, loyal and grey
Always ready to play.
Comes and sleeps on my bed
And on my knee there's her head.
She's not like any other dog,
Although the tree is still her bog.
Doesn't like the vet,
But she's the perfect pet.
I couldn't live without her,
There's no other puppy I would prefer.
Likes to eat a lot of food,
Which to me is pretty good.
She's a mischievous one,
Plus most of the time she pongs.
She's full of fun and love
I hold her toy up above.
She's the perfect pet for me.
Hee, hee.

Izzy Saint (9)

Funny Farm

Newborn little kittens,
Nana knitting mittens.
Hunting horse,
The police force.
Delicate bats,
Without their hats.
Danger dogs,
Sitting on logs.
Raging rabbits,
Children's habits.
Foggy frogs,
Jumping jogs.
Shiny sheep,
Lucky leap.
Cheeky chicken,
Kentucky fried chicken.
All the friends at the farm,
The farm goes off, with an alarm.

Jessica Moore (10)

Midnight

The tiger prowls through the long grass,
As the clock strikes midnight,
He sneaks silently along the stream,
The fish hiding in fear of his claws.
His long tail swishes and sways through the air,
As his ears pick up the slightest sound.
In the trees where he patiently sits,
Waiting to pounce.
His teeth are long and sharp,
His eyes seeing for miles,
His nose, as sensitive as a fingernail,
His balance, perfect, as he hops from branch to branch.
As the clock strikes 8,
The children laugh and shout, 'Tiger's home!'
As the midnight tiger, their beloved pussycat,
Returns from his adventures in the night to his biscuits.

Ellie Abbey (11)

My Cat, Meggy

Meggy has white paws and a black head,
She's as cuddly and furry as my big ted.
She loves to sleep,
And really loves to eat,
My cat, Meg.

She loves to lie in the sun,
But she weighs a ton.
She has an almighty purr,
She has a lot of fur,
I love my cat, Meggy.

Emily Rose Whitworth (11)

Polar Bears!

As the polar bear clung on for dear life
The velvet black eyes faded with fear
As he watched his only hope melting near
The sun rose rosy in the east
This betrayed the lonely beast
A solitary snowflake drifted gracefully
Then a crack, a cry, a crash . . .

Ella Bromwich (11)

Fandosey Dabbey

My dog, Abbey, is my best friend,
Although when I'm tired she sometimes
Drives me round the bend,
You can tell she's going old cos
Her fur is really grey,
She's a crazy dog really but she looks OK.
Just like my friend's dog, Loie,
She really is quite dumb,
Cos once I threw a ball and instead
She chased my thumb!
But apart from all that up there
She's still little baby Abbey,
And as well as that up there to me
She's Fandosey Dabbey.

Sarah Driscoll (11)

My Dream Pet

My dream pet has a fluffy tail,
A round pink nose and can climb over rails.
My dream pet is so furry,
Two beady eyes and can run in a hurry.
My dream pet has one small mouth
Likes to run and likes the south.
My dream pet sits on a mat,
My dream pet of course is a cat!

Sarah Pearce (9)

Crazy Dog

C uddly dog called Jaws
R an on all four paws
A ll furry and black
Z any and old, but never slack
Y es, that's my dog

D ances and likes to jump
O n a field he loves to bump
G osh, that's my crazy dog!

Phoebe Morris (9)

Animals

Some animals live in the trees,
Some animals live in the seas.
Some animals can sing,
Some animals are captured in cages.
Some animals can jump,
Some animals are happy.
Some animals are sad,
Some animals are soft.
Some animals are big, some animals are nasty.
Some animals are greedy, some animals can fly.
Some animals can crawl, some animals are good,
Some animals are being chased.

May To (8)

Terrific Tigers

T igers have the biggest paws
E agerly uses its long claws
R oars to communicate
R eady to pounce using its mental state
I t sneaks and creeps towards its prey
F earsome predator can eat all day
I nstantly, tigers can mark their territory
C an all this be mentioned in a tiger's life story?

T iny tiger cubs stay together
I n a group like birds of a feather
G ames can be rough
E ven though cubs can be tough
R eady for anything that's linked
S hame tigers are becoming extinct.

Save tigers!

Chloé Morris (11)

Animals In The Wild

Animals, animals, out in the wild, which one would it be?
Animals, animals, out in the wild, which ones would we see?
Animals, animals, out in the wild, you're sure to see at least one.
Animals, animals, out in the wild, some are super fun!
Animals, animals, out in the wild, you'll see them everywhere.
Animals, animals out in the wild, sometimes they'll give you a scare!
Animals, animals, out in the wild, whatever will we see this time?
Animals, animals, out in the wild, we'll watch them as the sun shines.
Animals, animals, out in the wild, some often climb trees.
Animals, animals, out in the wild, birds and bears and bees.

Jenny To (10)

The Feisty Eagle

The mighty bird has no fear,
He shall attack to protect,
Whether his prey is far or near,
He'll catch it with no neglect.

Get him to fly and spread his wings,
Watch him swoop around the trees,
Don't interfere because he's the king,
So no disturbing him please!

Be free feisty bird, just fly!
You amaze me by your skills,
Show us your talent in the sky,
We'll watch you from the hills!

Rasha Vadamootoo (11)

My Cat's Day

The golden sun is shining down,
On my cat's fur that is light brown.
Every morning he likes to eat,
Lots of fish and lots of meat.

The golden sun is shining down,
On my cat's fur that is light brown.
Every hour of the day,
My little cat likes to play.

The golden sun is shining down,
On my cat's fur that is light brown.
My little cat likes to rest his head,
On the end of my comfy bed.

The golden sun was shining down,
On my cat's fur that is light brown.
My little cat is sleeping tight,
Through the darkness of the night.

Laura Harvey (10)

Big Cats!

The tiger stalking in the night,
Gives all the animals a real fright.

The leopard prowls far and near,
Hunting gazelle, zebra and deer.

A pride of lions in the distance,
A lame ostrich needs some assistance -

Hunters look for animal fur,
Which makes the jungle animals stir -

So a puma scares the hunters away,
Leaving the cubs to frolic and play.

Ellie Mumford (9)

In The Jungle

In the jungle you can find,
Animals that can twist your mind,
Brown, red, blue and green,
Animals that are a joy to be seen.
Orange, purple, black and white,
Animals that can give you a fright.
Endangered ones - tigers, bears, apes and bees,
Take some time to think of these.
What can be done to protect all them?
If you know the answer, tell us please!

Iona Ferguson (8)

Dogs!

Fat dogs, flat dogs,
Like-to-chase-the-cat dogs.

Sleepy dogs, weepy dogs,
Living-in-a-tepee dogs

Hairy dogs, scary dogs,
Dressed-up-like-a-fairy dogs

Light dogs, white dogs,
Ones-that-like-to-bite dogs

Brown dogs, clown dogs,
Always-wears-a-frown dogs

Mad dogs, bad dogs,
Ones that look quite sad dogs

Lazy dogs, hazy dogs,
Smelling-like-a-daisy dogs

Slippy dogs, yippy dogs,
Belonging-to-a-hippy dogs

Silly dogs, frilly dogs,
Has-a-name-like-Billy dogs

Poor dogs, more dogs,
Sleeping-on-the-floor dogs

Posh dogs, slosh dogs,
Really-needs-a-wash dogs

Long dogs, wrong dogs,
Likes-to-howl-a-song dogs.

Some dogs are big, some dogs are small,
But my dog Scamp is the best of all.

Maisie Elizabeth Geobey (11)

I Love Animals

Awesome animals,
Big or small, sometimes they are short or tall,
How many can you see?
It might just be a buzzing bee.
I love them all and so do you
So let's have an animal hullaballoo.

Sophie Grant (8)

Olivia Octopus

Olivia is great,
Always working hard.
She is my marvellous mate,
Sure to send me a card.

She fills me with joy,
Everything she does is so clever.
Around her I'm never coy,
She'll be with me forever.
Olivia Octopus!

Stella Lily Fisher (8)

Animals

If I could be an animal
I would be a fish
I could swim around the ocean
And give my tail a swish!

I could chat to all the sea horses
Explore amazing caves
I could play with all the bouncy dolphins
And listen to the waves.

I could have tea with gentle turtles
And laugh like we were great friends
I could watch out for the deadly sharks
I never want this to end!

But when I am feeling tired
And I have to return to land
I will change into a human again
And be glad for who I am. *Me!*

Aoife O'Toole (12)

Queen Polly

(In memory of Bertie Bunny who died on 11/9/10)

Pretty Polly pussycat,
Lies purring on my bed.
Bertie Bunny lives outside,
Hiding by the shed.
Sometimes they are the best of friends,
And sometimes they are not.
But I love both my furry pets
Ever such a lot!
Polly is as black as night
And acts like she's the queen.
Bertie he just thumps the ground,
Whenever she is mean.
They are both so cute and cuddly
And make me smile and sing.
Without my pets in my life,
It would be soooo
Boring!

Rebekah Hopper (8)

The Queen Bee

Yeah, I'm the top, I'm the very, very best,
I always wear my yellow stripy dress,

Go and get some pollen from the flowers and trees,
For I come first, yeah, I'm the bee's knees,

I'm so jazzy, the wasps fly away, my antenna so snazzy as I fly all day,

The ladybirds hide as I glide through the grass,
spiders gasp as I pass, pass, pass,

I rule this jungle from bottom to top, no you can't
stop me when I'm on the hop,

I know you anywhere I can see you anywhere,

I'm the hip hop, tip top, preen, Queen bee!

Grace Tower (11)

My Dog

My dog is adorable
I want him to stay
With me forever
Until my last day

He sleeps on the sofa
And watches TV
When he is scared
He stays close to me

He waggles his tail
As if to say
I want to run
And play all day!

When he sees his friends
He jumps up and down
And bounds round the house
Knocking everything down!

I couldn't live without him
He is too wet!
We can't be apart
For he is my pet!

Georgia Humbert (10)

Seals

Seals are smooth, also sleek.
Seals jump for their food high in the sky.
Seals are always happy,
Though you can never tell why.
Seals are always dancing,
Underneath the sky.
Seals always crinkle their nose,
If they smell fish.
That's why I want to be a seal.

Charlotte Orriss (12)

Cheeky Hamsters!

Hamsters are so very cute, they like to run the wheel.
Some are extremely small and furry is how they feel.
I have two hamsters and they're the best two I've met.

Chloe Saunters (9)

Do You Mind?

I say, do you mind?
I say, don't you care?
That it is frightfully rude
Just to stare?

I know I'm a beauty,
An amazing feline,
But really this staring
Is quite out of line.

It's OK to look,
Not to shout, 'Look at that!'
But I suppose I am
Quite a gorgeous cat.

But still do you mind?
You don't seem to care
That I have already told you
Not to stare!

Ama Mae Henman (9)

The Cheetah

Swift,
Vicious,
Carnivorous,
In the family of cats.

Its prey,
Spotted,
Eyed,
Watched.

With the cheetah lurking
In the grass its prey's got no chance.

Now the cheetah is doing his dance
Because he can eat today.

Oh happy day! - that's for the cheetah
Of course, not its prey.

Jessica Grace Martin (10)

Silver Flash

I have a little pony,
His name is Silver Flash,
And when he is excited,
Boy you should see him dash!

His favourite treat is polo,
Though he just loves to eat.
When he sees apple and carrot,
He thinks, oh! what a treat!

He is a star, he learns so fast,
And everyone agrees,
He is my friendly, big best friend,
Silver Flash the pony!

Iona Molyneaux Townshend (8)

Little Doggy

Little little doggy,
Is bigger than you think,
It crawls on four,
Like a little, little froggy,
But can still do much more.

It can jump,
It can run,
Higher and faster than you expect,
Because any little doggy,
Is bigger than you think.

So cute, so small,
You should love it with your heart,
Snuggle in tight,
Because the little, little doggy,
Is bigger than you think!
Woof!

Ee Von Foo (10)

Dogs!

Oh dogs!
It's a pity they don't like mogs.
But nonetheless,
I think you'll agree,
Dogs are the best thing any thing's ever been!
The collies, so elegant, so swift,
The poor dogs in fights who get biffed,
The hunter coming through the door,
The Springer spaniel racing down the hall,
Dogs, dogs, dogs, I love them all!
I've two dogs, one called Trudy, an old dog,
And Mollie who's 8/10s blind,
And every dog, every kind,
I like each one that I find!

Phoebe Haywood (9)

The Mountain Eagle

The evil beak and dreaded talons
That clasp the scuttling prey.
Feared by most and respected by others.
Tethered to its mountain peak
Where its offspring lay.
Many dangers it will face,
Many an animal it will see.
A king, a hunter, it will remain,
The king of all birds,
The eagle.

Emma Caro (9)

My Bengal Tiger

You fascinate my mind
You live so far away, but yet it feels like you are right beside me
You're found in very few countries
You are loved my Bengal tiger
Could this be the reason that you are endangered?
Everybody wants you to be part of their life,
Be it in a zoo, in movies or even comic books, in picture frames,
Screensavers, worst of all some people would even wish to put you
On as a coat, or even stuff and place you in museums for display.
White tigers, as others refer to you, your strength amazes me,
Your blue eyes are like the sea that casts a spell of calmness in my mind
Your appealing pink nose is like the sun setting, absolutely sensational
Your creamy white fur is like vanilla ice cream
Your stripes make you stand out in a crowd
I imagine, you feel so soft, fluffy and warm to touch
If we were to be friends I would feel safe with you
I would always stand by you, and have a shoulder to cry on,
We would go swimming together because I know you love swimming
We would go hunting together because you're a good hunter
My Bengal tiger, as your secret admirer, I would find it very difficult
To forgive anyone who could harm you for whatever reason.
Though you may not pick me from a crowd my wish for you is,
To see you strolling majestically in your own world with less to worry about.

Paula Wanjiru (9)

My Purrfect Pet

Out of all the pets I've ever had
I have to favour one.
She never scratches and it makes me glad
To see her go about in her run.
Her paws are small and delicate
Her face is cherub sweet
Her fur is soft and fluffy
And it smells of hamster treat.
I just gave it away there
Or had you already guessed?
My purrfect pet
Is my hamster
And I think she's the best!

Rosalyn Sword (12)

The Puffin

Hidden in its mountain nest,
Left in peace to finish its rest.
Before the morning hours dawn,
It soars through the clear skies,
Bringing food where the new chicks lie.
Alone in their secluded fortress,
On the high grassy cliff top.
Their family in absolute harmony,
Away from the shadows of any darkness.
As the world is a changing place,
Who knows what, in the future, they will face
But sleep there knowing birds must,
As a new day is dawning and the sun is waking.

Ben Caro (11)

Hay, Racks And Igloos

As I sit on the slide and look at you,
I feel the love, I do, I do,
When I think of you, I'll never feel sad,
Honolulu, your hair is totally mad,
Giselle, your ginger fur is the new fashion,
Cappuccino, food is definitely your passion,
Merry, the oldest of the lot,
Guinea pigs, my hugs with you can never be forgot.

Amelia Fletcher (12)

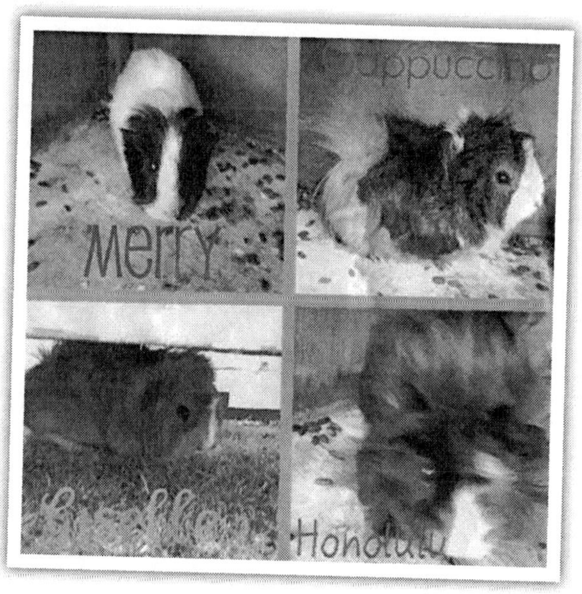

My Cat, Garfield

My cat, Garfield, has orange and brown striped fur.
She loves climbing my tree house,
Where she likes to catch a mouse or two.

She has a long slinky tail, and pink pointed ears.
She runs very fast and that makes me laugh.
Although she hates to take a bath.

She has silver-grey whiskers, and she's not very fat.
And she likes to sit on her special mat.
And then gets fed to her delight,
Then curls up in the silent night.
With eyes that glow all through the deep blue night.

Marc Canning (8)

Flower The Meerkat

There once was a meerkat
That had the name Flower
She lives in the Kalahari Desert
And she thinks she has power.

Flower lives with her family
And she has four litters a year
She has lots of sons and daughters
Like Tosca, Sophie and Shakespeare.

Every morning when the family get up
They go foraging for things to eat
They eat scorpions and scrubs
They don't really like meat.

When it's evening
The family go home
Then they start grooming each other
Without using a comb!

Julie MacLeod (11)

True Friend

As I get home I'm so happy to see
That little smile smiling at me.
You're my true friend,
My definite friend.
As I get back from school, I'm so happy to see
That little tail wagging at me.
You're my true friend,
My definite friend.
My life is a happiness with you near.
I don't know what I'd do without you here.
You're my true friend,
My definite friend.
        Lola!

Courtney Hillman (11)

Rabby Babby

Rabby Babby you are so fluffy,
And I love you so,
Even when your eyes go puffy,
Rabby Babby you dig so many holes,
That spoil our gorgeous garden,
But at least you're not a mole!
You thump the ground really hard,
With your tiny feet that hop and skip,
But you're still the best at sending cards!
Rabby Babby you're the best rabbit ever!

Grace Gregory (9)

The Red Pandas

T he red panda is shy and lives alone
H e lives in forests and you'll see him roam
E ating fruit, acorns and bamboo

R oots and eggs to name but a few
E veryone likes to see him climb
D evouring leaves most of the time

P andas, however, are becoming rare
A nd if we're not careful there'll be no bear
N umbers are declining every day
D esperately we want our friends to stay
A ll of us must help them right away!

Jack Caden (10)

My Little Bunny Called Hunny

There was a little bunny called Hunny
She liked to eat all the honey
And when she was done
She went for a run.
So that's why she's called Hunny Bunny.

I had a rabbit called Hunny
She was very, very funny
And when she died
I cried and cried
'Cause I had lost my bunny called Hunny.

Jodie Latimer (11)

Tia Maria

Black soulful eyes,
Thin muscular thighs,
Cleverly hidden ears,
A face that shows no years,
A cute small nose,
No fingers or toes,
Soft scaly skin,
Blue eyelids that are thin,
No teeth and no lips,
And no visible hips,
A hard patterned shell,
Something I wouldn't sell,
She's a friend not a pet,
She'd never tall a secret,
She is my little girl,
My own special pearl,
I'm talking about Tia,
Her name is Tia Maria,
She cuddles without a purpose,
'Cause Tia is a tortoise.

Poppy Iveson (13)

Dexter

My brother is called Dexter
He's always there for me
Lots of cuddles every day
He never sends me away

My best friend is called Dexter
He really is the best
Always ready to play
He never wants to rest

My dog is called Dexter
He's the best that's ever been
Cute and fluffy madly scruffy
What else could you want from him?

Dexter is everything to me
He makes our family complete
So much love to give
I wish that you could see.

Eryn Alexandra Blount (10)

Gus

I had a friend called Gus with a tail to wag,
She liked to sleep on my sleeping bag,
Gus loved to sit in the truck with Dean
Although that was when he was nice and lean.

Down the track we walked side by side,
With Gus loving those on who she relied.
Companion, friend, confident and routine,
Oh, how Gus will be missed by Dean.

Albany Milton (10)

Oh Bruno

My sweet little puppy Bruno is so cute and black,
He doesn't even bark.
But as the days went by he got bigger and bigger and still didn't bark
Then one day when we were out he saw his friend down the lane
And through the excitement he barked a very loud *bark!*
So now I have a big cuddly friend who only barked once, *oh Bruno!*

Scarlett May (7)

Animals

Animals, animals
What lovely creatures,
Some of which have
Beautiful features.
Some are big,
Some are small,
Some are little,
Some are tall.
Some are scaly,
Most are furry,
Some are hissy,
Some are purry.
But in my eyes
Animals are cool
And they also
Totally rule.

Nicole Joseph (12)

Lions

Lions are beautiful,
With coats as golden as the sun,
They sleep when they are full,
The cubs have lots of fun.

Some lions are white,
And have very good eyesight.
Male lions have almighty roars,
While lionesses do all the chores.

Jessica Toase (8)

Manatees - Water Cow

Manatees are slow,
Not as pretty as a pink bow.
Not as thin as a movie star,
Not as expensive as a fancy car.
But they are in need,
So they can resume their life in amongst the weed.
They are clever and smart,
They have a big harmless heart.
They live in warm water,
They swim beside their son or daughter.
They are there waiting for your love.
Not to be injured by the boats above.
Protect the waters where they live,
To give the manatees the home nature did give.

Rachael McCracken (11)

Saffy

I had a cat called Saffy,
But she ran away
Her eyes were such a piercing green
Her fur was charcoal grey.

It made me sad to think,
Why did she have to leave?
We loved her very dearly
Her absence is hard to believe.

She used to bring us breakfast
Rabbits, birds and mice.
My mum used to shout and say
That wasn't very nice!

Saffy has a new house
I'm so glad to say
She lives with my granny and grandad now
So we visit her any day.

Sacha McMullan (11)

Dopey Diesel

Diesel is a dopey dog,
He runs and darts about.
Then he starts to chase his tail,
Until he's tired out.

Jordan Graves (8)

The Silent Wolf

He looks up towards the moon
Asking himself how much longer he would have
Before dawn would be upon him,
Looking all around him
He slunk silently and swiftly
Towards his target
Without a breath, he pounced
A mouse lay dead in his powerful jaws.

Nicole Stringer (16)

The Snow Leopard

These beautiful, majestic creatures
With gorgeous, glistening fur
Their huge great silky paws
And their booming loud purr
Living up in the icy mountains
Where they can run free
Cold, so cold but they love it
Might not be your cup of tea!
Their teeth so white and shiny
As strong and tough as lead
Except after they've made a kill
Then their teeth are stained red.

The big cats are dying
From humans poaching for skins
These wild animals aren't pets
That eat canned food from tins
You can't tame them, parade them, show them
Like some little fancy cat
They can't be kept in zoos
Or be in cages, trapped like a rat
Try to help in every way
If you don't want the animals to die
We don't want to destroy these amazing creatures
Are you really ready to say goodbye?

Megan Gisborne (14)

I've Always Wanted A Dog

Even though my mum says no,
I've always wanted a dog
I see a tiny dog outside my window,
I watch, I cry,
And wish I could have my own tiny, little dog,
Any dog would do.

Emily Eldridge (11)

Our World

Please don't pollute our sea
It is home for my friends and me
Splish splash splosh
The shoals of fish and coral reef
When we look down they're beneath
Splish splash splosh
Please make sure you are guided
To the bins that are provided
Splish splash splosh
We love to play where there's no litter
So the sea can stay a-glitter
Splish splash splosh
Please keep the sea clean for
Dolphins . . .

Emma Napthine (15)

Gardoo, Gardoo

Gardoo, Gardoo
You are flexible and cute
Your dark blue eyes shine in the light
They keep me safe in my bed at night
Your white milky fur is downy soft
Your walnut brown nose is like chocolate.

Gardoo, Gardoo
You play fetch like a dog
You are a Birman by breed
You pounce and bounce like a rabbit
You are very smart indeed
But most of all Gardoo, I love you.

Sophie Ihiaifar (9)

My Best Friend

My dog is barking
Like he always does,
He loves walks
Around the block,
He just wags his tail
When he says, 'Yes please.'
He'll do anything
For his daily meals.

He sits in his bed
All day long,
And when I ring the bell
He tods along,
When I open his food bag
He comes to see,
My best friend is my dog
And my dog loves me.

Luke Herrington (13)

I Love My Hamster

I love my hamster

L illy is her name
O ut of all the other hamsters she's the best
V ery loving
E veryone loves to hold her

My friends want her
Y ou would love her

H er cage is pink
A nd she loves it
My hamster loves sweetcorn!
S o that's why I love her
T he cutest hamster of all
E very day she goes in her green ball
R olling round and banging into things!

Maisy Mitchell (11)

Fluffy The Rabbit

He's furry and cute
But also very mute
He's the best friend I've ever had
And now I'm really rather glad

I really, really trust him
I really, really love him
I really, really adore him.

He's fluffy and jumpy
He's very, very snuggly
I love him very much
And he lives in a hutch.

He's the best rabbit in the world
He's not even very old
He's very, very bold
And he doesn't get cold.

Lauren Hemmings (8)

The Dragonfly

Indigo, green and violet sheen,
With grace that I have seldom seen,
In reeds and water lurks the queen.
Her wings, ornate and webbed so fine,
A fabulous work of nature's design,
She's the sweetest, simply divine.
She skids across the silvery lake,
Leaving the frail, droopy willow in wake.
There is much to be done and no time to take.
She darts like a laser, slashing the fog
Stealing a fly from a moody brown frog,
Keen to return to her rest by the bog.
Into the forest, a maze of tall trees,
Her dainty wings whisked away by the breeze,
Until, in the distance, the dragonfly sees
A tranquil place to sleep with ease.

Maria Dempsey (12)

Aye-Aye

Skittering, leaping,
From branch to branch,
In the bathing glow,
Of the bright, cold moon.

Under twinkling stars,
On a warm summer's night,
A creature unknown to the world,
Went sneaking.

A pair of gleaming black eyes,
Peeped out from the foliage,
A long, bushy tail and small pricked ears,
Moved excitedly in the wind.

The Aye-Aye is nocturnal,
Slinking about in a black fur coat,
With long, long fingers and exceptional balance,
It is by far the most unique.

A cheeky smile spreads across its pixie face,
As it continues on its way,
Unheard of to any human,
A secret born to the Earth.

Skittering, leaping,
From branch to branch,
In the bathing glow,
Of the bright, cold moon.

Under twinkling stars,
On a warm summer's night,
A creature unknown to the world,
Went sneaking.

Jana Isabel Craddock (12)

Penny Chicken

Penny chicken loves spaghetti,
Penny chicken loves the corn
Penny chicken is the quickest
Racing round the lawn.
Penny chicken drives me dotty
Her feathered coat is so spotty
She's not the tallest in fact the smallest
How I love you, Penny chicken.

Darcey Mae Noakes (11)

Little And Large!

I adore every horse,
And guinea pigs of course,
Cute guinea pigs,
Gnaw on apple wood twigs,
Soft fur coats,
Horses munch on oats,
Guineas in a hutch,
Horses don't care much,
Where they're kept,
As long as their stall is swept,
Guinea pigs look above,
Give them your care and love,
Horses are quick,
Although they might kick,
A guinea pig can be quiet,
But they do enjoy salt wheels so buy it,
They don't barge,
However horses charge,
Beware little and large!

Teri Trevains (10)

Crazy Dolphins

Dolphins, are so crazy
Dolphins, they aren't lazy
Everyone adores them
So why do we ignore them?
I think that they are so cute
I think that they are so wild
You never know where they will pop up
You never know where you'll end up
I think that dolphins are so crazy
But I don't think dolphins are lazy.

Cara Louise McQueen (10)

Horse Love

I remember the sound of his thudding hooves
I remember how swiftly his body moved
One day he'll come galloping back to me
And it will be love, that we will soon see.

His name is Twister, he's the one I love
He's a horse, sent from above
I remember the day when he was sold
I remember how I cried, for he was like gold

But whatever you love, will soon be sold
Out in the streets, or out in the cold
Your heart will be broken, so like mine
But as long as it's in your heart, it will be fine.

Lucy Alexandra Robertson (9)

Barney The Boxer

Barney the boxer is a muscly chap
He likes to go for a walk and play with bubble wrap

Barney the boxer is your playtime bud
When you see him sleeping give him a hug

Barney the boxer is like a child
He likes to go on the park and go absolutely wild

Barney the boxer is my all time favourite pet
I love him to bits dry or wet!

Brittany Moore (11)

Awesome Animals

Cats and lions, tigers and bears,
So many animals in the wild air.
Some eat chickens, some eat fish,
Some eat acorns and out of a dish.
All of them rustling in the leaves,
When suddenly they find a swarm of bees.
They run and they jump and chase wildly!

Awesome animals
Rustling through the leaves.

Zaynah Hussain (8)

Between Wolves and Men

Why does Man kill the wolf?
Is it because he doesn't understand them?
Is it fear or maybe jealousy of something so beautifully free?
Or did Man see himself within the eyes of the wolf
And loathe the thought of being compared to a mere beast?
If so, then why has Man invited the wolf into his home
As his forever faithful companion?
The wolf walks by Man's side, always has and always will,
Until the very end of time.
And when it does end,
You can bet that the wolf will still be at Man's side by choice.
Man will welcome the wolf then, when all has turned to nothing,
And the only comfort is the patient watchful guardians of our homes.
Why does Man kill his saviour, his companion, his friend?
The fates of wolves and men have always been entwined,
But sadly it will take disaster for Man to see what has always been there.
Please help stop the murdering of wolves before it's too late.

Katie Tavender (15)

My Favourite Animal - Tapir

In the jungle there is an animal,
That not many people know about,
Its name is a tapir,
And it's my favourite without a doubt.

I love its adorable appearance,
Its ears and very long snout,
Its big body of soft brown skin,
You can't miss it when it's about.

I love the way it moves,
When there's no danger around,
So slow silent and unrushed,
It holds its head so proud.

I love the tiny calves,
With the stripy and spotty backs,
So full of life they jump and leap,
Just like a jumping jack.

I love the way it relaxes,
So peaceful without a care,
As it snoozes I want to stroke it,
And its tuft of soft brown hair.

I love the way it swims,
To cool off in the heat,
Diving down for aquatic plants,
That it will eventually eat.

But the thing that makes me sad,
Is that tapirs are endangered,
And it also makes me mad.
So find out more about tapirs,
And maybe you will see,
Why tapirs are special and they mean so much to me.

Katherine White (14)

Pandas

Pandas are so cute, I send them all my love,
But it's such a shame that their forests are being crushed.
Pollution and poaching are causing this threat,
And very soon the pandas will be dead.

Pandas are cuddly, but big and bulky,
It's like a teddy bear version of the Incredible Hulk!
There are about 1600 left in the wild,
Why do people's love have to be so mild?

I hope my affection never ends,
And when I'm older, I want to help to defend.

Jade Gaute-Brown (12)

The Cute Little Cuddly Cub

The cute little cuddly cub playing by the trees,
Round and round he goes racing through the breeze.
This cute little cuddly cub runs to his friends,
As he has discovered some tasty looking hens.
They scratch at the fence and try to get through,
But there is nothing in the world they can do.
Now it's almost night-time,
Snuggle up safe and sound,
Tomorrow will be another day of playing around.

Bethany Louise Child (12)

C'mon And Help The Rescued Pups!

They're from RSPCA, Dog's Trust and all the other ones you can think of,
They're all the same, they're not the ones to blame,
It wasn't their fault they were in there,
The owners were cruel and selfish and mean to let their
dogs go through such dismay,
Not worrying about what other people would say,
But now they're alright, they are bathed and cleaned,
Brushed and cut to make them look puppy perfect for
their new owners to collect them.
When they're collected they're taken to their new home
With new owners who are nice and kind
And hurting the dogs is the last thing on their minds,
They are now looked after and cared for,
Never ever hurt by anyone anymore,
They have comfy beds and clean toys and very yummy food,
We can't do anything to stop them being chucked out,
But please do your bit and help us out,
By coming to the rescue centres every once in a while,
Could maybe save the lives of some of these poor, innocent animals.
Do your bit and help save the dogs and puppies!

Ella Mary Austin (11)

Goodbye Rosie

My pet, Rosie, was a lovely dog
Taking her for walks in the fog.
She liked the snow the best,
And once we bought her a green vest.
She chased other cats but not our own,
Everyone knew Rosie, she was well-known.
She was loving and funny and bouncy and clean,
My Rosie was never ever mean
But the years caught up with my faithful friend
Visits to the vet were near the end.
Now she is in Heaven and I miss her so.
I know she was poorly, she had to go.
So goodbye Rosie. RIP.

Natalie Hughes (10)

My Perfect Pet

Pets are there to help you,
To comfort you and play,
To make you feel all warm inside,
For you to treasure every day.

Pets are very loving,
They're caring and so kind,
They'll have a special bond with you,
That's very nice to find.

Now Tyson is my lovely dog,
My soft and cuddly pet,
My furry friend, my perfect pal,
We make a great duet.

He cheers me up when I am down,
He really makes me smile,
Spending time with Tyson,
Makes everything worthwhile.

Tyson is my favourite pet,
The one I love the most.
My special bond with Tyson,
Is what really makes us close.

Shannon Stones (12)

Endangered Species

When everyone is finished school for a year,
They all come out to shout and cheer.
It isn't all that happy for some,
For the big melt has come.
Up in the Arctic and down in the Poles,
Animals come out of their hidey holes.
Knowing that they have less land,
The thought every year isn't so grand.
For most Arctic animals are in danger
And the problem is becoming pretty major.
For when our great-great grandchildren finish their last school year,
These amazing animals might not be here!

Shaun Flynn (10)

My Kitty Cats

My kitty cats
Are grey and black,
They always mess around,
But sometimes when they're sleepy,
They like to snuggle down,
My cats can be so lazy,
When they lay around,
In front of the TV
Why aren't they running around?
They are very soft and cuddly,
And like lots of company,
I love my little kitty cats
And hope they love me.

Adele Maher (9)

Galloping Horse

His golden tail swishes and sways freely,
Glistening in the sunlight,
While he leaps around happily,
He gallops and neighs loudly all day long,
And when he needs a drink he will slow down to a steady trot.
When it's a wet day, you will see sadness in his face,
His eyes will be filled with tears which makes his elegance fade away.
His face is very long as he starts to kick and shout in his mind,
He doesn't like very wet days because he can't go out to play,
He's mainly chestnut brown but he wishes he was black
Like the friend in his dreams.
He never had a friend to run and play with,
His hopes of having a friend dropped
So he stood there in his stable, the animal we all love
The galloping horse.

Hannah Elizabeth Raine (10)

My Pet Cat

My pet cat was called Jo-Jo,
She had never made a foe,
When she wanted to play,
She would use your lap as a tray,
She would roam across the floor,
Then she would scratch at the door.
She would always have something to share,
Until she fell off the chair.
I will always miss her so,
And she will always be my pet Jo-Jo.

Carter Whitby (11)

The Tiger

Your granddaughter comes up and sits on your knee,
Then she says, 'What were tigers, why aren't they here for me?'
It's a very sad tale,
One of humans' biggest fails.
A tiger was an elegant creature, beautiful too,
Precious to the likes of me and you.
They heard the chainsaws, gunfire and deadly shouts,
We knew they were going without any doubts.
But we didn't care,
We were too wrapped up in our own affairs.
They all went, one by one
Till we couldn't count how many had gone.
There were adverts, begs and protests too,
But no one really knew what to do.
But then the last one was dead,
'So that's the story,' I said.
I saw the look upon her face,
Was there nothing we could have done to save that amazing race?

Katie Rose Coverdale (11)

My Loveable Pets

I have a dog, Nala is her name
She loves to play her favourite game
Chasing the cat round and round
Until she pins him on the ground!

I opened the door, Nala flew out
Running around and prancing about
The next thing I know, she is eating the snow
At ten times a go!

Squiggy loves the heat
You can hear his heartbeat
If you didn't know
Squiggy's my cat
And I love them both so!

Ebony Nicole Elliott (12)

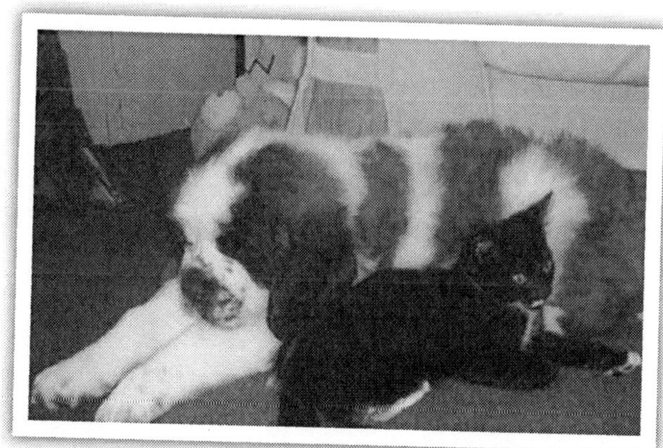

Dogs

Dogs love their walks
And their squeaky toys
They are also girls' best friends
Not just the boys.

They are friendly and playful
And love to prance around
They are like a spring box
Never have all four paws on the ground.

Making new friends every walk
Well see them again tomorrow
And when we don't see them
We both feel full of sorrow.

Siân Mary Davies (12)

RIP Del Boy

Del Boy my budgie, you were so fine,
So fragile and timid, but you were mine,
You weren't just my friend, but Rodney's too,
But one day you looked ill, I wondered what to do.
I took you to the vet, as she shook her head.
'This doesn't look good,' she strictly said.
I got a bit worried, but still had faith,
As we took him home, where he was safe.
A few weeks later we let him out the cage
As he fell to the floor with a flood of rage.
Tears filled my eyes, watching him die,
Goodbye Del Boy, as he closed his eyes . . .

Sunny Andrews (11)

Zac

My pony is my bestest bud,
He always gets covered in mud.
He does enjoy a favourite treat,
Sweet, sweet carrots to eat.

My Zaccy is such a dream,
He wouldn't think of being mean.
His favourite thing is to jump,
We try not to land with a bump.

So I, Esme, am here to tell,
What my Zaccy does so well.
In competition he's hard to beat,
Because the judges think he's so sweet!

Esme Owen (10)

Busy Guinea Pigs

They scurry around cute and furry,
Always seeming like they're in a hurry,
This way and that way,
Forwards and back ways,
Grabbing this, nibbling that,
Gosh you are such busy chaps,
First you're chewing away,
Then you're huddled in the hay,
I wonder what you'll do next,
Because you're charging round like you're T-rex,
Don't be stupid, don't be silly,
You're just my cute little guinea piggies!

Jennifer Audrey Milne (13)

The Group Of Three

(This poem is based on my three loving cats, Sally, Alfie and Gizmo)

The group of three are mischievous,
The group of three are loud,
The group of three are distinctive,
The group of three are proud.

The group of three make you smile,
Although you know
It's not worthwhile.

Ben Robinson (12)

My Circus Rabbit!

The blue-grey ball of fluff is Skye,
She always has a crazed look in her eye.
When she is happy, she kicks her legs high,
Prancing around the garden.
Big brown eyes and a white nose,
When she sees a camera all she does is pose!
She chases and jumps over the ball
And when she hides for fun I call, 'Skye! Where are you?'
Popping her head out from behind the shed,
Her eyes open wide,
She performs a fanfare full of joy and pride!

Liane Macdougall (15)

Phoebe

Chasing after birds and basking in the sun,
These are the things Phoebe finds fun.
She hates loud noises and bright lights,
So she hides behind the couch on Bonfire Night.

She stares at the lions when they're on TV
And she wonders, 'Is that my cousin I see?'
But she runs behind the couch when they roar,
So I think she would prefer to stay in her bed behind the door.

She loves to eat fish
But I think meat's her favourite dish.
When my mum throws away a tuna tin,
She tries to get some by staring at the bin.

I love stroking her soft fur,
And listening to her adorable purr.
While she sleeps next to me
With her head rested on my knee.

She was playful as a kitten, but now she's getting old,
So I have to be careful with her, I've been told.
She's around the age of seventeen,
So if she needs to run around, she is not so keen.

Fiona Martin (12)

My Special Zebra

I have a guinea pig whose name begins with B
He always eats apples and loves to nibble me
He looks just like a zebra even though that's plain to see
I love my little guinea pig, he is called Blackberry!

Abigail Proctor (13)

My Pets

My rats, Rhubarb and Custard, have long tails
Y ou can stroke them rough and smooth

P urring cats, Percy and Charlie
E ating their food in a hurry on the slide
T otally loveable Rosie dog
S wishy tail and fluffy paws.

Mary Allison (7)

Dolphins!

D ancing majestically,
O ut and in,
L eaping from azure waters,
P laying joyfully,
H appily smiling,
I ntelligent creatures,
N oiseless hunters,
S pecies sadly endangered!

Natasha Jade Young (9)

A Tiger's Day

Roar! The tiger went while entering the long grass,
Hungry the tiger was.

Grrrr! The tiger watched his prey,
Sneaky the tiger was.

Silently, the tiger went while slowly creeping forward,
Stealthy the tiger was.

Noisy the tiger was as he leapt out to his prey,
Focused the tiger was.

Violent the tiger was when he bit his prey,
Successful the tiger was.

Bang! Went the hunter's gun,
Scared the tiger was.

Panicking the tiger was as he ran all the way home,
Safe the tiger was.

Sleepy the tiger felt as he softly fell asleep,
Lazy the tiger was.

Tara Catherine Byrne (12)

Dolphin

Fast and elegant,
To and fro,
There's the dolphin,
Off she goes.

Her skin seems smooth and delicate,
Her eyes twinkle and shine,
She cuts the water as she dives,
Sometimes I wish she was mine.

She hears through her skin and teeth,
To sense for danger far and wide,
She loops the loop like a roller coaster,
She always leaps out and does not hide.

Please stop hunting land or sea,
This wonderful creature must live and be,
Let her live with all her friends,
I want to save her, that's what I'll be!

Fathima Ra'ana Riyaz (11)

Yum, Yum, Yum!

I lie still and don't peek,
When dinner comes I will
Sneak, snap! Yum, yum, yum!

Lying still in my camouflage,
None can see me, I'm quite large,
Lick! Yum, yum, yum!

Sitting down on a rock,
I lie asleep in my frilly main frock,
Bite! Yum, yum, yum!

I lie by myself on my own,
I somehow smell bone,
Munch! Slurp, slurp, burp!

Amy Coleman (11)

Fantastic Dolphin

F un in the sea
A nice rush
N o more water fun
T wo fins help to swim
A friend to play with
S omewhere in the blue
T urtles play with them
I wave goodbye
C ome back soon

D otty dolphins in the air
O n the way
L oving its food
P laying in the sea
H igh in the air
I n the water
N ot many left.

Emma Charwin (7)

My Animal Is My Best Friend

My animal cuddles me when I am sad,
My animal is there for me when I am mad,
My animal cheers me up when I feel bad,
My animal is my best friend.

My animal holds me tight,
And can sometimes give me fright,
My animal stays by my side,
My animal is my best friend.

My animal is so sweet,
He loves to eat and eat,
My animal hugs me at night,
And I know he will never leave my side,
My animal is my best friend.

Rebecca Suzanne Talbot (13)

My Turtle

My turtle is green one day and purple the next,
He is a bright jolly fellow that has a great smile,
He has a red tongue that pokes out on the left side,
My turtle is 12 and is very sweet!
He loves to play darts and many other sports!
My turtle likes to eat rats and play all day long,
I love my turtle and he loves me!
Wait . . . I think he does!

Emily Rickets (10)

My Shadow

Shadows in the sunlight
Shadows in the dark
But the best one to me
Is the one right here.

He's a big ball of softness
Inside and out
With alert, enormous ears
And fluff still from birth.

A tail so long
You won't know it's there
Until he yelps
Then settles elsewhere.

If you meet him
You'll be greeted with a friendly lick
Others shouldn't worry
'Cause he'd never leave them out.

How lucky are you
To be one of his favourites
He'll rush to see you
With a loving kiss, cuddle and shake.

If you're at the end of his lead
You'd better hold tight
Or if not
You'll go for a flight.

Through bushes and gardens
To trees you'll go
As he chases a cat, squirrel or rabbit.

He's a dog
Fair and square
And he's very handsome.

But which breed?
People may be surprised
That my big softie
Is an adorable German Shepherd.

Katie Jade Neocleous (10)

Night Stalker

Elegant predator of the night,
Bird of prey, on its flight,
Spread its wings, watch it go,
How to fly, it will show.

Silent stalker of the night,
Eyes like diamonds, shining bright,
Watch out world, here he comes,
Wise old creature, claws instead of thumbs.

Through the night,
Past the trees,
Night-time stalker, comes to me.

Natalia Almeida (12)

Elephants

(Elephants are my favourite animal but unfortunately they are endangered!)

E lephants are my favourite animal
L arge and lovely
E motional and elegant is how I describe them
P oor elephants are killed for their ivory tusks
H eavy and huge are other words for them
A nd harmless is
N ot just an opinion but also a fact
T hey are always friendly and
S imply sweet!

Ruhi Shah (11)

My Stick Insects

S omething brown and stick like
T hey look invisible
I nsects that look like sticks
C rawling up the cage
K eeping very still

I like them walking up my arm
N ot leafy
S hed their skins
E at bramble and ivy
C laws that hold on
T rying to hide.

Sophie Brown (6)

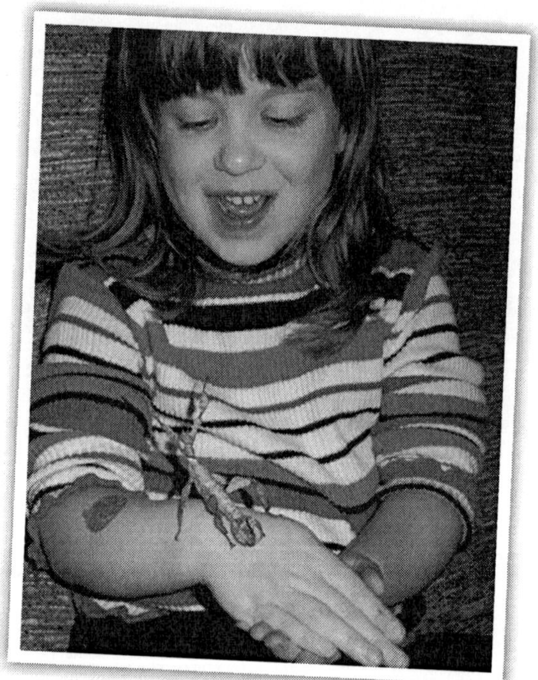

Untitled

The lithe sleek shape
Its body twisting through
The long grass
In pursuit of a shadow in its mind.

As the small body turns
A bush rustles almost silently
Ears are pricked
Eyes tighten with a longing for the chase.

Suddenly, the air goes still
Its paws lift high and pad down slowly
Whiskers tremble and heart quickens
The small body comes into sight as the moon shines.

Heidi Leigh (12)

Benjamin

He has a favourite T-shirt,
It's stripy blue and white.
He wears it all the time
Although it's getting tight.

He enjoys his Sunday lunch
Especially the meat.
He also has biscuits
For a little treat.

He really is a messy one -
Gets gravy everywhere!
He's ultra energetic
For a guy with white hair.

But don't get me wrong,
Sometimes he's a sloth!
He really can't be bothered moving,
That's till he sees a moth.

I wouldn't say it's stinky
But he has mighty meaty breath.
He likes to run and jump on things
And scare them half to death.

His hair is something special,
It's very soft to touch.
He hates it when you brush it
'Cause he thinks he's rather butch.

I can tell when he is coming,
I can hear a tip-tap-toe,
Sometimes his voice is squeaky,
Sometimes his voice is low.

He wants to be an archaeologist,
Well, that is what I found.
For when I went outside,
He'd dug up half the ground.

He's a bounding white ball of excitement,
A really special friend.
I know he'll always be there for me,
Until the very end.

He's a real curious George
Although his name is Ben
And he pinches things around the house
And puts them in his den.

Ben's a little Westie.
Have you gathered he's my dog?
I'd read this poem to him,
But he's sleeping like a log!

Antonia Nicole Kelly (13)

Untitled

Majestic, he is the king without a title,
Eternally moving in his cousin's shadow,
And though he hunts with a graceful stealth,
They are in awe of the grandeur of his kin's kill.

He may weave through the grass as water through a river,
But his beauty is overlooked by the roar and splendour
Of his maned relative, who rules by tooth and claw,
Who stands on his pedestal, raised above the crowds.

Overlooked by all but those who hunt
With relentless greed, a life for money,
A fair exchange? And so, as the sun gazes
Across the plains, shots are fired

The regal beast falls. Death looms, watching while
Life flickers like a flame. Moments, brief moments
Before the darkness reigns. One thing remains,
Petty death for petty trade.

Kelly Schweizer (15)

My Cat, Magie

A killer, murdering the innocent
Mischievous, vicious and cruel
A liar, a cheat and a bully
A minx, mean and nasty
A predator spying,
Sly, cunning and devious
Picking out the weakest
Getting ready to pounce
In one moment, it's over
He's horrible
Creeping up and down his home
Marking his territory
Shining, his luminous, bright eyes
Vile creature
But he's very cute and fluffy!

Aja Cristabelle Dodd (13)

Leopards

Leopards hiding in the long, wavy grass, hiding for its prey,
Camouflaging so no one or nothing can see them.
They laze under the trees, blocking them from sunlight.
They play around sometimes even though they are wild,
Save the leopards and help them live.

Trinity Lam (10)

My Cat, Charlie

My cat is cute,
My cat is silly,
In bed he likes to lick my toe.

My cat is soft,
My cat is funny,
My cat follows me wherever I go.

Rhiannon Pope (7)

The Piebald Veteran

His mane flows in the remarkably bright sun
He runs with his friends - the chestnut and the bay
He gallops, it looks quite comical
The piebald veteran watches on, in the cold wind of April.

Rain falls down, it's April showers
He runs around, like he's the star of the show
The trees do a pliè, not long before the horses run underneath them
Shelter is what they need and it's the best they'll find.

He argues with the chestnut, his nostrils flare
The squabble comes to a conclusion, they're friends again
He glances towards a mare in another field, she whinnies back,
The veteran thinks he's extremely juvenile.

Not one of the other horses know that the veteran is an ex-racehorse
How he wishes to gallop around with the others
But he is ageing and his joints are sore
He knows that he used to act childishly like my horse!

Eleanor Hardy-Dearness

Scorpion - Just Treatment?

Sting
Clawing
Other words for . . .
Running, screaming
Passing out at sight
It has no friends and no home
On the other hand it does kill
Not at best cuddly not kind or caring
So what? Humans burn, kill the scorpion.

Jacob Selby (12)
City of Norwich School, Norwich

The Liger

The liger is a crossbreed cat of a lion and a tiger.
Its stripes are faint,
Its fur's like paint.
Its teeth are as white as pearls,
If it jumps on you it'll make you hurl.
It's a very, very friendly cat,
It's a mix of this and a mix of that.
They feed it 50kg per day,
It makes a nest in a bundle of hay.
It weighs 50 pounds,
It's lightning fast on any ground.
Fortunately it lives in a zoo
It couldn't hunt a cow that goes moo.

Jack Rushworth (12)
City of Norwich School, Norwich

Preciously Endangered

Purrfect, perplexing, perilously in danger
Pussycats at heart
Predators on the outside
People prefer them as skins and cloaks
Poor lions, prefer their cubs not as fur coats
Profoundly in danger because of this hunt
Peace is their wish, together as one.

Purring, roaring, emotions they show
Perfect for them, their wild home
Pleadingly they claw at their zoo cage doors
Playing on the savannah is where they should be.

Please, please, help our wildlife
Protect not exploit
Donate today to someone who,
Will help our lions get back under the sun.

Tasha Nelson (12)
City of Norwich School, Norwich

The Great White Shark

As powerful as Zeus,
The great white shark rules the beautiful open ocean
With massive eyes this vicious beast can see anything.
As the pinky plankton tries to sneak past this ginormous creature with teeth the size of rocks,
The shark darts like a thunderbolt trying to catch its prey,
It sways in and out the rocky reefs in the amazing and magical sea.
It circles its prey then eats it in one.
Thank goodness sharks live in water,
That's why you never see a shark in a park.

Oliver Connor (12)
Clayton Hall Business & Language College, Clayton

The Vulture

He darts and dashes to his destination
To try to get to the rest of his nation.
He zooms and zooms across the land
Creating terror where he stands.
Crushing bones and eating the marrow inside,
If I were a small animal I would hide.
He eats every last bit of skin
So he doesn't become thin.

He 'caws' noisily throughout the jungle,
He calls so loud the ground must rumble.
All the animals that hear his cry
All hide away, he says, 'Don't be shy.'
His body built like a terminator
Ready to hunt and kill ya.

If you see one will you wail?
This is the end of my vulture tale.

Ross Edward Taylor-Hamlin (11)
Clayton Hall Business & Language College, Clayton

My Cat

Lotty is my cat
She is very fat
She waggles her tail
She's a bit of a whale
My little puss loves a fuss
And when I go to bed at night
She's there before I turn out the light
So in the morning when I wake up in bed
She's always there lying by my head.

Hannah Sweeney (11)
Clayton Hall Business & Language College, Clayton

My Guinea Pig

Slow or fast he can go
Trot or gallop he can also you know
Like a cheetah he can crawl
But he's not as fast as I recall.

Munch, munch, munch is how he eats
It bites so fast it must quicken his heart
First a dandelion leaf then some grass
Give him some fruit and he'll never pass.

He has big pink ears and a small nose
Since I first got home, my, he has grown
He has petite paws and is black and white
He has lots of fur but he's still light

So that's my guinea, cute and small
I hope you know about them more than before.

Emma Crick (11)
Clayton Hall Business & Language College, Clayton

It's A Dog's Life!

And the dog ran round
In the slushy, muddy ground
Splashing and splashing
Sprinting and dashing
She charges towards the birds
Like a mass of buffalo herds
The dog barked aloud
Unable to fit in with the crowd.

She gobbles up the food
Like she's in an eating mood
Crunching and munching
Slurping and burping
She drinks the water speedily
But not so much greedily
Chunks of food fly out the bowl
But most will fill her empty hole.

She soars through the grass
Like a cheetah in attack
Barking and growling
Groaning and howling
She looks excited like she wants to play
Her tail wagging as if to say
It's time to play . . . hip, hip, hooray!

Meg Whalley (11)
Clayton Hall Business & Language College, Clayton

The Beauty Of The Ape

With his humongous hands
He hits his chest
As if to say
'I'm king!'

The mammal leaps through the trees
As light as air
With an enormous swing.

Big leaves, tall trees
And the sound of croaking frogs
Birds singing, apes swinging
But no sign of smelly hogs.

He has his best mates
Alligator and Snake
And that's the beauty of the ape!

Kyra Pashley (11)
Clayton Hall Business & Language College, Clayton

My Dog

She sits outside and loudly barks
Even in the garden and the crowded park.
She caught the massive ball flying
And the little boy started crying.

As her food is coming, like a moon she waits
In the garden by the old rusty gate.
She quickly gobbles it down in one whole
Straight after that she digs a deep hole!
But after all that she is the best
Amazingly better than the rest!

Emily Barclay-Hill (11)
Clayton Hall Business & Language College, Clayton

The Dragonfly

As he flew around the animals hid
With his silky wings beating around him
He dived down and *bam!* The fly was gone
That's the dragonfly's trick number one.

He sat there patiently waiting for food
No one would recognise him if he'd moved
An unlucky fly flew past him close
Then his tongue flew out and the fly was food
That was the dragonfly's trick number two.

He flew low around the pond
He was looking for something but you couldn't tell what
His head went down in two seconds flat
Then his head came up looking satisfied
That was the dragonfly's trick number three.

Chloe Hulme (11)
Clayton Hall Business & Language College, Clayton

The Scorpion Sting

He scuttles, searching for his prey
Hoping for some meat on that scorching day.
His shell gleams like a crystal jewel
He's found his prey, it is a fool.

He paralyses it with his sting
It bled to death, the giant thing.
He eats it up, piece by piece
The scorpion deserves this mighty feast.

He eats a bit but gets full up
So his colony comes and finishes it, bottom to top.
They head back to their underground tunnels
And as night comes, they make a huddle.

James Bailey (11)
Clayton Hall Business & Language College, Clayton

The Dog

It creeps and crawls around the field
And gallops and jumps through the grass
Once it galloped like a mad horse!

Once it ate like a terrifying tarantula
Didn't chew its food, just gulped it down
If you don't feed it you are going down!

It sniffs and snorts all day long
It has an almost unreal bark
It always growls at other dogs.

It lives in a silent green garden
With a little red robin for a friend
This may seem odd, it's my dog!

Nathan Purchase (11)
Clayton Hall Business & Language College, Clayton

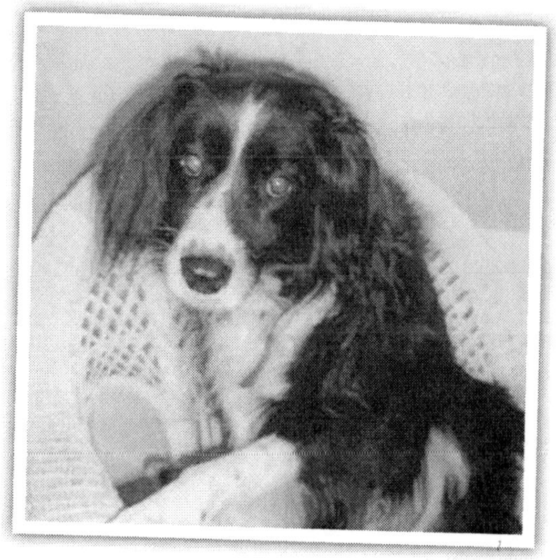

Toto

My little Toto
He may be small but he's never wrong.
My little poodle
But his heart is what is really strong.

My little hero
When he gets excited he's more hyper than a kid on Christmas Day.
My little prince
And when it's bathtime he'll always break away.

My little troublemaker
His fur is an apricot colour, almost gold.
My little friend
As long as I live he shall never be sold.

My little puppy
What a funny entertaining and wonderful friend.
My little dog
He will be faithful until the end.

My little warrior
He's hardly subtle, he'll never make 007
My little fighter
Being with him is like being in Heaven.

My little Toto
He may be small but he's never wrong.
My little poodle
But his heart is what is really strong.

My dog, my Toto, my friend,
I'll always love him.

Eva Hobbs (11)
Clayton Hall Business & Language College, Clayton

Love For Louis

My little Lou Lou
As cute as can be
He likes to rest his head
Upon someone's knee.

It's calm and quiet
When he isn't around
And when he's asleep
There isn't a sound.

He is very greedy
And loves to eat
But when he's a good boy
We give him a treat.

When he's bored
And alone all day
When I come home
He wants to play.

With his bushy eyebrows
And his wagging tail
I know my love for Louis
Will never fail!

Grace Clarke (11)
Clayton Hall Business & Language College, Clayton

Alfie, The Dog

He is as rabid as a squirrel when he sees a new face
When he's upstairs he darts for the pillowcase.

In the colourful house he lives
In the day he's active chewing everything in sight.
At night he's a pain, begging for food
And at 7 o'clock his head is like a clock waiting for his treat.
In the morning he waits for his mates before he is left alone.

James Shuker (11)
Clayton Hall Business & Language College, Clayton

Monkeys

They stand still so you think they are statues
Eating bananas, fruit and vegetables.
They screech as loud as they can to deafen your ears.

They run with the wind on their front and back paws
Swiftly swinging from tree to tree trying to keep out of danger.

They lived in a friendly zoo
Covered in fresh, green grass and tall dark trees
They go outside to sleep and to spend more time with their family.
They play joyfully on the play area happy as can be.

Georgia Hanley (12)
Clayton Hall Business & Language College, Clayton

The Blue, Blue Kingfisher

He stunningly glides through the crisp autumn air,
Landing effortlessly on his oak river branch,
Waiting like a teenager, for their GCSEs,
And when his golden moment comes,
Boy, does he take it;
He dives carelessly at the cool, crisp water,
His call a warning to the golden river salmon,
The blue, blue kingfisher ain't goin' anywhere.

As majestic as he may seem,
A violent brute is just as common,
And boy, is he a lot better,
Kicked up a notch he dives like lightning,
Catching his prey,
Yum, yum, yum, what's for tea?
Just one more time ain't very likely,
Cos the blue, blue kingfisher ain't goin' anywhere.

And when the night does eventually come,
He still waits, to fill his red tum,
The heart warming, soul wiping kingfisher,
Never ever rests,
His last perilous food dive,
Is a big surprise to the sleeping river salmon,
And as long as his oak river, branch still stands,
The blue, blue kingfisher ain't goin' anywhere.

Connor Nixon (11)
Clayton Hall Business & Language College, Clayton

The Falcon's Hunt

When the crucial moment comes,
The raging dive comes out to play,
To clutch unwary new prey,
But now that prey can never play.

Now the prey is long gone dead,
The short sharp beak will sink in dead meat,
So you wouldn't mess with the falcon before it's fed.

When its meal is done,
It will soar for fun,
But now it retires until the next day dawns.

When the next day dawns,
So does the falcon,
When you hear the high pitch screech,
As it bounces off the mountain rocks,
Your end is near.

Marcus George Latham (12)
Clayton Hall Business & Language College, Clayton

The Grizzly Bear

Don't trespass in the cave,
Otherwise you'll meet your grave.
He is a very tough animal guarding his dome,
If you dare go near, he'll make you run home.

Strong, sensitive, keeping the beat
Stomp, stomp, stomp with his heavy padded feet.
His teeth are showing in the light, so get out of his way
Otherwise he might kill you, in less than a day.

He's very caring to his family,
Looking after wife and baby cubs.

Alisha Edwards (11)
Clayton Hall Business & Language College, Clayton

Silent But Deadly

He floats and waits for his unlucky prey,
Camouflaged into the deep blue,
His razor-sharp teeth waiting
Slowly to strike,
Silent but deadly.

First very slow, then a fish with a nerve swims by,
Hoping, praying that the predator won't spot him,
But sadly he does.
The fish is scared, the shark is speeding through the blue,
The fish gets away,
Silent but deadly.

The hunt starts again but now
It's a school of fish, easy for the shark.
He watches the school then he strikes,
His jaws are wide open,
Snap, shut, end!
Silent but deadly.

The sea murky and blue, wavy and stormy on top,
But calm underneath.
Until the shark comes, you watch out,
Because when you're underneath,
When you see the king of the waters,
Your time is near.

Josh Snow (11)
Clayton Hall Business & Language College, Clayton

Lion

Sitting tall and proud in his very spot,
Waiting for prey, patient he is not,
A roar as loud as a jumbo jet,
It started raining and he got wet,
He shook the rain from off his fur,
He strolled away with a mighty purrrr,
He though he saw a bit of food,
So he started to get in a hunting mood,
Slowly he crept after the treasure,
He hoped tonight he would have some pleasure,
Chew, chew, crunch, crunch.
Imagine tucking into that lunch,
The lion dreamt of having a feast,
He started getting closer to this beast,
The lion watched this lovely bush deer,
Strolling quietly trying to get near,
Jumping and pouncing on this little mite,
He would scratch and bite to win the fight,
Now that he has got his plan,
He needs to stand up and be a man,
The lion walked away in shame,
Knowing that he would have to take the blame.

Mathew Eagles
Clayton Hall Business & Language College, Clayton

The One Day Death

As the mighty lion woke up next to meat which was raw,
He heard a vulture with a frightening caw.
The lion ignored it and carried on with the new day but
Feeling strange . . .

The troubled lion went past the forest where trees
Are turned into books,
Past the smelly, babbling brooks.
When the lion carried on he spied his first prey of the day,
He slowly stalked the slimy snake,
Pounced. Eaten, not as nice as cake.

Then a loud bang came from nowhere
The lion shocked, gasped for air
Rapidly he looked around
And slowly fell to the ground.

As the lion slowly dies, thick blood in his hair,
The vulture comes back, circling around him in the air
The beaked hunter let loose a horrifying caw
The lion screamed his loud but last roar.

Alastair Scott Clarke (12)
Clayton Hall Business & Language College, Clayton

Untitled

My dog races like a car,
Eager to go,
Ready to tear.
He runs
As fast as lightning.
He eats
As quick as a flash,
Gobbling, gulping and churning for more.
He doesn't bark, he lets out a roar,
Sending a shiver down my spine.
If he's not pleased, then he lets me know
He ignores my commands, or when I say no
He lives in my bedroom,
That was the deal,
He tears away at my books
Leaving them in shreds.
I take him for a walk
To calm him down
But he drags me
Across the floor
100 miles an hour!
In the park,
He charges around
Like a bulldozer,
Big ears flopping over gouging eyes.
He is unconcerned he causes havoc
All around him
He never stops to sit and pause
He sees everything as an assault course.
Standing tall and mighty
As proud as a lion
He's not divine
I wish Angel wasn't mine!

Louie Bester
Clayton Hall Business & Language College, Clayton

Dolphins

Jumping in the air,
Gliding through the oceans,
Forever searching for food in the shimmering sea,
Following the boats to see the people who greet them with a smile,
That's a
Dolphin's life for me.

The shiny coats,
Their playful days splashing in
The waves,
People try to catch a glimpse
Of their exciting ways,
As they surf
Along the water with their heads held
High in the air,
A dolphin's life for me.

They must be careful of the many dangers
At sea,
The sharks, the nets, and the people that dive
To take a look at the sea,
Beware dolphin that they don't catch you,
A dolphin's life for me.

The shiny coral,
The crabs on the bottom of
The sea,
The flash of cameras when they
Have an uninvited visitor,
That's the life of a dolphin under the sea for me.

Stephanie Johnson (12)
Clayton Hall Business & Language College, Clayton

Jaguar!

Fast, speedy, slick,
Camouflaged in the mist it waits,
For a sign of movement.

Accurate, powerful, deadly,
Its teeth as sharp as a sword,
Just waiting to pounce . . .

Surrounded by forest it waits,
Then suddenly pounce,
And it's all over for the prey of the jaguar.

Connagh Brookes
Clayton Hall Business & Language College, Clayton

Falcon

A falcon is my favourite bird
That flies so high or so I've heard
It feeds on pigeon, plucked from the sky
As it swoops so fast like the blink of an eye
It lives on rooftops of buildings so tall
With its eyesight so keen it can see it all
Its squawk can be heard for miles around
Which scares the pigeon when it hears the sound
But silent is the deadly strike
Then back to the nest for a little light bite.

Scott Cooper (11)
Clayton Hall Business & Language College, Clayton

Meerkat

Leaping and lurching,
Burrowing and bounding.
That's the way the meerkat moves.

Nibbling and gnawing,
Ripping and tearing,
That's the way the meerkat eats.

Squeaking and screaming,
Squawking and shouting,
That's how the meerkat speaks.

Grassy and sandy,
Tranquil and quiet,
That's where the meerkat lives.

Jonathan Sharman (12)
Clayton Hall Business & Language College, Clayton

Elephant

I'm an elephant as huge as can be,
My trunk is so long to reach up the trees,
I walk very slowly due to my size,
Swishing my trunk from side to side,
I live in Africa a country so hot,
With my huge floppy ears and eyes like dots,
When I run I make the ground shake,
I am the size of the Empire State,
I'm quiet and silent like a mouse,
Using my trunk to feed my mouth,
I love eating leaves and nuts and fruit,
I am so handsome, gentle and cute,
I may be built like the size of a house,
But see how fast I run if I see a mouse.

Ellie Ann Leverton
Clayton Hall Business & Language College, Clayton

Paparazzi Pet

My pet his name is Xypytotex, he has more glamour
Than Posh and Becks.

He likes to zoom left and right,
And he watches my bed for safety at night.

He is a real lazy bones, him and his mate Colin,
Beggin' for stuff, so I have to go shoppin'.

Even though he is very minute, he pulls a face
That is so, so cute.

He may be small but he has got a mighty bite,
Quick as a rocket zooming in mid flight.

When he gets stuck he wiggles with a splish,
You couldn't have guessed that he is a fish.

Jordan Greener (11)
Clayton Hall Business & Language College, Clayton

The Eagle

It stands regal
It glides like an aeroplane
It soars like a kite,
The eagle
It catches its prey with eyes so bright
It hunts day and night,
The eagle
It flies fantastically
It glides gracefully
It catches prey like a sitting target
The eagle
Its claws are like knives
Its eyes are like the sun
It's terribly terrifying,
The eagle.

Daniel George Ratcliffe (11)
Clayton Hall Business & Language College, Clayton

Snake

Sleek, slender, secretive, the snake slithers
And sneaks.

Stiff, discreet, camouflaged,
Coiled, hidden away, he seeks.

Hot, misty, murky
The warning sounds from the jungle.

The deafening sounds of an elephant's rumble,
Hundreds of mice stampede in a pack,
Now time for the snake's satisfying snack.

Anna Leonard-Dunn (11)
Clayton Hall Business & Language College, Clayton

My Best Friend

My best friend is different to you
As he runs very fast
He loves his chews
He'll shake a paw to greet you
Into his warm and clean home
He races around playfully until you sit down.
Then finally he falls to sleep,
But if you move he will peep.
After a while he starts to rile,
Sly and sneakily,
He moves up and down the property,
Quiet as the pinching puppy.
He will move room to room looking for some things to chew
Until you find him.
There is no clue.

Molly Lawton (11)
Clayton Hall Business & Language College, Clayton

Christmas Present!

Loud as an amplifier,
As quick as a lightning bolt,
Soft as a furry cushion,
Colourful like a parrot.

Splodges, sharp teeth and a massive jaw,
Small, cute and cuddly,
Grey and brown,
This is my Christmas present that's come to town.

She lives in a cage high on a drawer,
With bits of wood that came from a saw,
A solitary creature that needs toys to play,
This is my hamster I feed every day!

Robbie Garland (11)
Clayton Hall Business & Language College, Clayton

Badgering Beak!

She ruffles her rainbow feathers high up on her perch,
The forest chatters and shrieks with unseen diverse,
She casts a weary coal eye around the umbrella-like canopies,
Daring an intruder to terrorise her territory,
Shuffling along her bony fingered branch,
She launches into flight, and just by chance,
At the exact same moment the forest is still,
The ball of warm humid fire kills,
The loneliness and shadowiness with spine-tingling light,
She truly is feathers in flight,
She glides and roams through her tranquil home,
Singing and chatting like a chimpanzee
And every animal appears from their homes,
To listen to her beautiful badgering beak!

Caitlin Ball (11)
Clayton Hall Business & Language College, Clayton

Fred The Fearless

The garden stood still until the predator roamed the grass,
First he gave the blackbird the fearsome death stare, roared
Like a lion and ran at the blackbird like a cheetah racing at a lost gazelle,
Furry, fuzzy, Fred walked proudly with his prey, dropped it in
The kitchen and went to get the tired mum.
Mum was not happy, she shouted at fearsome Fred
But a minute later he was asleep on her legs.
Fred wasn't scared, Fred wasn't worried, watch out birds
Because Freddie's coming . . .

Dylan Hawkes (11)
Clayton Hall Business & Language College, Clayton

About A Dog

My dog's as cute as a cupcake
Happy as the sun
Soft as silk
Always playful and fun

Wise as an owl
Sly as a fox
Fast as a Ferrari
Strong as an ox

Brave as a lion
Bright and bold
Cuddly as a teddy bear
Has a heart of gold.

Bethany Hickman (11)
Clayton Hall Business & Language College, Clayton

Safari

Driving slow, through the African bush,
What a rush, it's so lush.

Heat blazing, antelopes grazing, it's amazing!

Cheetahs running very fast, dashing past, don't be last!

Giraffes so tall, with babies so small, I'm having a ball!

Lions roar, birds soar, I want more.

Trunks swinging, tails flinging, my heart is singing.

By the pool, getting cool, watch out, lions! Don't be fooled.

Driving slow, here we go, what a show!

Elicia Thompson (11)
Clayton Hall Business & Language College, Clayton

The King Of All Birds

He's the lightning in the sky,
He's the bullet in the trees,
Swiftly scanning for its next victim,
The sparrow hawk locks on and
Descends its blow onto its victim like a nuclear bomb.
So for all those reasons the sparrow hawk rules.

Alexander James Chapman (11)
Clayton Hall Business & Language College, Clayton

Snake

It hides in the long grass, hissing,
Waiting for its prey.
It lies there slithering,
All night and day.
It lies there waiting,
For movement in the hay.
And with a blink of the eye!
It lies there smothering,
In its snake only bay.

Fraser Perry (11)
Clayton Hall Business & Language College, Clayton

The Giraffe

Roaming the open grasslands,
He is a silent peaceful giant.
The tallest of all animals,
The skyscraper of the savannah.
He looks down on the rest of his world.

Standing on towering legs like stilts,
He owns an unique dappled coat,
Spotted like a leopard.
With his stretched slender neck.
He reaches to eat from the treetops.

He travels in herds with an ungainly gallop,
Using his excellent eagle-like eyesight,
He scans the scorching hot lands,
If predators dare to approach,
He strikes with a killer kick.

Natasha Yelland (11)
Clayton Hall Business & Language College, Clayton

A Loyal Friend

With a wet black nose and a long black tail,
A dog's cuteness is never going to fail,
Prancing about in the long green grass,
Getting everyone wet as they pass.

With black fur as dark as the night sky,
You will always know when they go by,
From slobbery tip to a waggly end,
You always know that they're a loyal friend.

And at the end of a good day,
They will still come and play,
Because they're always there for you,
And I know this is to be very true!

Rebecca Jade Twardochleb (11)
Clayton Hall Business & Language College, Clayton

Hunting Tiger

Lurking in the trees,
Among the morning mist,
You were prowling.

Deep in the Asian forest,
Where the antelope were grazing
And the warthogs were paddling,
You were waiting.

Lurking in the trees,
Among the morning mist,
You were prowling.

Seeing the antelope
Grazing in sight,
Not knowing what you were planning,
You were waiting.

Lurking in the trees,
Among the morning mist,
You were prowling.

The forest filled with light
As you leapt and caught your prey,
You ran into the forest again,
And then . . .

Lurking in the trees,
Among the evening mist,
You were prowling.

David Sillitto (11)
Clayton Hall Business & Language College, Clayton

A Man's Companion

Howls like a kettle,
Races like a sports car,
Competes like an athlete,
Growling like a hot rod,
Hunts like a tribesman.

A man's best friend,
A cat's worst enemy,
A faithful friend,
A blind man's eye,
A policeman's deputy,
Anything's eater,
And a hider's seeker.

A dog is a friend,
A dog is gracious,
A dog is faithful,
A dog is a helper,
A dog is playful,
A dog is a buddy,
A dog is very muddy,
A dog is fun.
When my dog is good
I give him a bun!

Peter Dobson (11)
Clayton Hall Business & Language College, Clayton

Simply The Best!

Unique, majestic mammal, walks alone at night.
If you see him in the foggy forest, he'll give you all a fright!
Big, scary, it isn't fair,
No one stands a chance against the big grizzly bear.

Fast, agile, deadly as a snake,
He will tear and shred you apart, it isn't fake.
Ravenous, muscular, like a tiger he bounds,
Stamps his way through the cold forest, you should hear the sounds.

Hungry, brutal, sits by the stream,
His razor-sharp claws at ready, in his eye there is a gleam.
Intelligent, clever, he knows what's coming next,
Eating his prey with his sharp clawed paws, his teeth as sharp
as the ones on a T-rex!

David Oprescu (11)
Clayton Hall Business & Language College, Clayton

White Fish

My goldfish is a funny character,
because he is not actually gold!
He has actually turned white now,
because he is getting old.
He still has fun in his tank,
swimming up and down.
I think he is my number one pet,
and for that he deserves a golden crown.

Every now and then he will see me come in,
then swim up to the side.
I look at him,
then he hides.
When I go to bed he waits until I see him,
then he starts to dance.
I have missed one thing out I'm sure,
Oh yes, his name is Lance.

Alexander James Walne (11)
English Martyrs School, Leicester

Untitled

The illuminating fur stood out under the sunlight
Its eyes were orange and its skin was pale
The animal's fur felt smooth
Its indulging stripe was scarred from fights
His orange eyes stood out as I looked at him
As he had a background of jail
His tooth stood out white as chalk
But I also knew he could bite
I took another look at his gold soft fur
As peacefully he went and laid
It was a great big tiger all covered in fright.

Roberto Roseman (12)
English Martyrs School, Leicester

My Dog!

My dog is a groovy kinda dog
His tongue is like a slippery mountain
With saliva always sliding
His ears are always flying
He's like Scooby-Doo crazy
He's also good with the ladies

My dog is a groovy kinda dog
He's as fast as lightning
And his bark is as loud as a lion's roar
He loves the adventures garden
He adores his family
And we adore him
Because he's the life and soul of our house
My dog Milo
One of a kind
And he's all *mine!*

Jared Rydquist (13)
English Martyrs School, Leicester

Orca

My animal is an orca whale,
Otherwise known as a killer whale,
It swims with such elegant grace,
It shares its magnificence all over the place,

The reason for its 'killer' name,
Is that it doesn't eat krill in shame,
They eat seals and fish for their prey,
When they're hungry they're not gonna play,

There's a film about one called 'Free Willy',
It is very famous, not at all silly,
The best thing about the orcas,
Are their brilliantly stunning colours,

Such simplicity of black and white,
Would win a rainbow without a fight,
It's such an awesome colouration,
Would certainly win any occasion,

Yes, my animal is an orca whale,
Otherwise known as a killer whale.

Dominic Fitzpatrick (12)
English Martyrs School, Leicester

I Love Zebras

I love zebras,
They're my favourite animal.
They spend most of their time eating grass
They do not like the smell of gas,
They are in the wild,
But if you are a child
You might see them in a zoo.
They come in groups
But they're not from troops.
They have a leader which is a male.
They have furry tails.
I love zebras,
They are my favourite animal.

Josephine Ann Agu (12)
English Martyrs School, Leicester

My Dog

Cute, small, black and white
With small tail and big eyes,
A really friendly animal,
What is it, what is it?

Loud but sometimes quiet, not small
Not tall but medium sized,
A pet that is always happy to be around!

A happy and intelligent pet
That is always running around.
What is it? What is it?
Is it a cat or rabbit? No!
It's a really friendly dog!

Julia Rurarz (12)
English Martyrs School, Leicester

Tigers are so awesome with their orange body and black stripes.
They are so fierce but friendly
and they are so cuddly.
That's why I think a tiger is an awesome animal.
Tigers are so wonderful in many ways
and they will always be there for you.
They will protect you from anything
if you have a special bond with it.
That's why I think a tiger is an awesome animal.
Tigers are helpful and cheerful when you are sad.
They will always stand out more than all the animals in the world.
That's why I think a tiger is an awesome animal.

Callum Hudson (12)
English Martyrs School, Leicester

Bunny Rabbit

I'm afraid of spiders,
I'm afraid of snakes,
I'm afraid of bees, the crocodiles in the lakes.
But above all,
I'm proud to stand tall,
to say a bunny rabbit
is my favourite animal of all.
It's fluffy, soft and very cute,
me and a bunny would perfectly suit.
I want one as a pet,
but my dad just won't let.
As sweet as I may look,
my dad says, 'Go read a book.'

A bunny's so cuddly and so sweet,
it's better than a bird that just goes *tweet*

So if you want to buy me a pet,
even though my dad won't let,
buy as a present, a gift you may say,
buy me a rabbit for me to play!

Aleshia Kelly (12)
English Martyrs School, Leicester

Dazzling Dolphins

Splish, splash, the dolphin screeches,
Splish, splash, she needs some friends
Don't worry we will help.

Splish, splash, the water is fun,
Splish, splash, there's work to be done,
Don't worry dolphin, we will help.

Splish, splash, I love dolphins,
Splish, splash, please sponsor them
Don't worry dolphin, I will help.

Maxine Kutinyu (12)
English Martyrs School, Leicester

Untitled

The big fur ball that is the mammoth
It stomps loudly, keeps close to the rest of the herd.
The alpha male stays in front, protecting the rest of the herd.
They find some food
When a group of human hunters leap out at them
The males attack, but the hunters are too agile.
The males are taken away, the herd scrambles.
The injured males chase off the hunters
An unsuccessful hunt.

Sebastian Wells (12)
English Martyrs School, Leicestershire

My Diesel

My big, clumsy, lazy black rabbit
Who is also my hungry, furry little friend
You live in a big brown hutch at the bottom of the garden.
You make me smile every time I look at you
Making me remember you're a part of the family
You're strong, fast and will never hurt a fly.
That's why I love you
You love it when I scratch behind your ear
Making you feel comfortable in my arms.
I love your name and it fits your colour perfectly.

You're free and awesome, that's why I called you Diesel.
Love you.

Ashleigh Hassell (12)
English Martyrs School, Leicester

Guess What?

He' soft and cuddly,
He's got white fur,
He's got a stripy head,
He's a big cat and big purrs,
He lives in Siberia.
Who is he?

Zach Cochrane (12)
English Martyrs School, Leicester

Peachy The Peach Dog

Perfect as can be,
Cheerful, full of glee,
Guard of the house,
She won't chase a mouse.

She's fierce but cute too,
Chicken that's what she chews,
I whistle, she comes to me,
We're great friends, that's what you'll see.

She's my cousin's pet, very sweet,
I like her a lot, but she likes treats,
Back then I was eleven,
But Peachy's from Heaven.

Peachy the peach dog!

Pamela Anne Yap (12)
English Martyrs School, Leicester

Fluffy Rabbit

Fluffy rabbit, fluffy rabbit,
Soft as snow
Fur as thick as a hedge
It only eats veg

You just want to cuddle
Every day and night
Looks so, so innocent
Everything a rabbit does is right

Last thing I need to tell you
If you do everything I said
You won't feel a bit scared
All you need to do is follow what you've read!

Tammy Pereira (12)
English Martyrs School, Leicester

My Auntie's Dog

My auntie's dog is small
fluffy, cute and ruins the living room carpets
and her name is Muffin.
My auntie's dog - Muffin barks like a pig
and loves going for walks and playing in the park.
Muffin loves everyone to pieces
no matter who it is.
And Muffin's talent is eating muffins
especially blueberry ones.
I love her to bits
I don't know what I would do without her.

Molly Colette McAuley (12)
English Martyrs School, Leicester

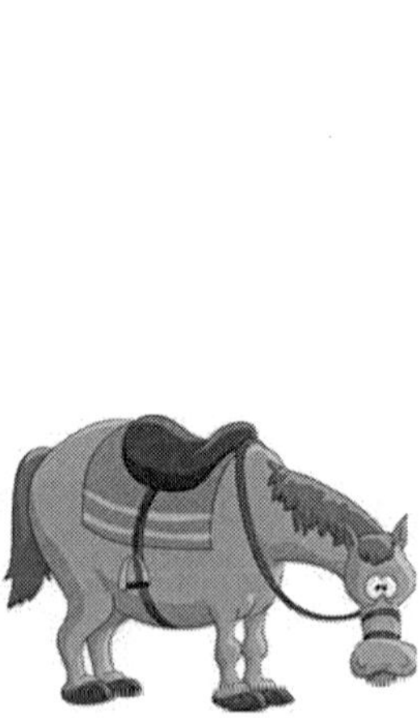

Fizz . . .

Long legs, sharp claws, pointy ears
she's got it all.
Running up and down the garden
doing back flips as she chases her tail.

Looking around the garden for a new trail
with white fur with black spots
and bright green eyes
she could never get lost.

In the night it is a fright
when you hear bangs and crashes
you look outside and there she is in the tree
so off I go down the garden
to try to get her out.
When she is off, I carry her back inside
then she follows me back upstairs
and falls asleep on the landing.

She is a muppet at times,
but she is still my cat
and I have her for that
my crazy Fizz!

Elena Brailsford (11)
English Martyrs School, Leicester

Jazzie, My Dog

The family dog,
is our little friend,
she always will be,
right till the end.
She is so energetic,
we wonder why,
even though she wouldn't,
hurt a fly.
She is very well trained,
we don't have to shout,
you've gotta be careful,
when Jazzie's about!

Isabella Owens (11)
English Martyrs School, Leicester

Bob The Hamster

Bob the hamster was fat and chubby,
Bob the hamster was playful and funny,
Bob the hamster was grey and white,
Bob the hamster would never get in a fight.

Bob the hamster was a fat little guy,
Bob the hamster was chubby in the thigh,
Bob the hamster would sleep and kip,
Bob the hamster might give you a nip . . .

But he meant well and he led a good life
Bob.

Lydia Picken (11)
English Martyrs School, Leicester

My Dog

He's soft and brown and a little bit round,
He's loveable and cuddlable and I never see him frown.
My dog, his name is Shadow,
The family pet he is,
At times he can be sneaky and also very cheeky,
He always keeps a secret and never tells a lie,
Playful is his middle name,
Especially when he's in the rain,
My dog he'll always be the same,
And that's the way I like him.

Jacqueline Naomi Ardron (11)
English Martyrs School, Leicester

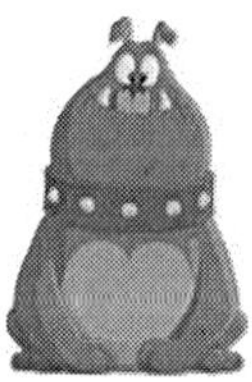

Leopards

Leopards, leopards are so fast,
When they run they will zip past,
If you ever hear one roar
I bet that you'll head for the door.
Leopards, leopards are so cool
They'll terrorise your entire school
And they are so very brave
That's why their lives are ours to save.
Leopards, leopards are so loud
You can hear them in a crowd
Leopard, leopard, I love you
It's a shame you're in a zoo.
PS: don't feed the leopards.

Shomari Potter (12)
English Martyrs School, Leicester

Dog!

A dog is nice
A dog is fun
He always wants to mess around
A dog is soft
A dog is relaxing
A dog can bite
A dog can smell
A dog is strong
It's man's best friend.

Eltrent Summers (12)
English Martyrs School, Leicester

I've Got An Unusual Pet

I've got an unusual pet
Her name is Kat
She is a cat

She jumps, rolls over, takes a dive
Up my back, onto my shoulder,
Hoping I would grab and hold her.
Then she jumps to catch a fly,
She's four months old, my sweetie pie.

She steals other pets' toys
Chips and chocolate are her joys
Her owner is a tiny boy
I call him Roy.

Her colour is like a fashionable dress,
So eye-catching, so beautiful.

She loves to dance to Susan Boyle.
Kat is so special like a royal
Kit Kat is her nickname
When they're playing a gambling game
My sister puts her to shame.

Every day at half-past six, she would wait to watch Garfield the cat
She loves to dress as the cat in the hat.

Sharon Mukombe (12)
English Martyrs School, Leicester

My Rabbits

My rabbits are so cute, just like a flute
They hop around all day long in a field they belong.

My rabbits are the best, better than the rest
They are happy, they are happy but they are simply the best.

My rabbits are so cool and not fools
They are a perfect make and they make me think of cake.
My rabbits are so cute, just like a flute.
They hop around all day long, in a field they belong.

Melissa Clinton (11)
New Mills School, High Peak

My Dog

I have a dog
It's a dim dog
It's a slim dog.

I have a dog
It's a funny dog
It's a lovely dog.

I have a dog
It's a silly dog
But it's my dog.

Tunde Bayode (11)
New Mills School, High Peak

I Want A Dog

I want a dog with a shiny black nose
I want a dog with a tail that goes

I want a dog that doesn't bite
I want a dog to sleep with at night

I want a dog that's black and white
I want a dog to cuddle tight

I want a dog but I haven't got one.

Philip Morley (10)
Ribbleton Avenue Methodist School, Ribbleton

Princess Penguin

My penguin is a princess,
She acts like one too.
She loves to wear dresses.
She loves make-up too.
She loves to sing,
And dance as well.

Chandni Chhohan (10)
Ribbleton Avenue Methodist School, Ribbleton

My Bunny Is So Funny!

My bunny is so funny
He lives down the alley with Danni.
My bunny lost his money, he fell over, bumped his head,
and went in a 1, 2, 3.
So my bunny is a dummy because he is so funny.

Adam Miya (10)
Ribbleton Avenue Methodist School, Ribbleton

My Dizzy Duck

I have a dizzy duck
Who likes to play and dance
She's got bright blue and pretty wings
A pink beak and purple feet,
She dances round and round
As glad as her beak
Jumps around as fast as her feet
At the end of the day
She goes, she goes *quack, quack, quack*
As lovely as she can be
Then she goes *quack, quack*
Waddling down the street
And in a house and *quack* asleep.

Kerry-Leigh Blythe (11)
Ribbleton Avenue Methodist School, Ribbleton

The Hamster That Is A Gangster

My hamster is really cute
And eats lots of fruit.
He wants to play.
Every day.
He plays in his ball
And that's not all
My hamster is a real gangster.
If you want to go faster
He is the hamster.
He eats pasta to go even faster.
He is the master.
If you want him you can't, he is my
Gangster hamster!

Dion Julia Hulton-Mcmanus (10)
Ribbleton Avenue Methodist School, Ribbleton

My Rabbit, Dopey

I had a rabbit.
It had a habit.
Of eating carrots.
That was my rabbit's habit.
Dopey was his name.
I won him playing a game.
And that's how Dopey got his name.

Muhammad Huzaifah (10)
Ribbleton Avenue Methodist School, Ribbleton

I Love Kittens

Kittens are the greatest
To me they are the best,
If there was a champion kitten
There would be no contest.

My uncle bought a kitten
And it used to tickle your feet,
I thought it was so funny
That I wanted to give it a treat.

Kittens are so energetic
And love to play outside,
I think they are so cute
And they love to take a ride.

Kittens are too my favourite
To me they are the best,
They play all the time
And they always treat the rest.

Amaarah Abid (10)
Ribbleton Avenue Methodist School, Ribbleton

The Cheetah

The fastest animal around,
In Chinatown,
In underground,
When he turns around he sits down.
He is a predator,
Hunting for the senator,
Always killing animals, doing it for his survival.
He is so smart his birthday's in March.
He is so cool he makes ya look like a fool.
He's far from a prey, he never has to pay.

Umar Patel (11)
Ribbleton Avenue Methodist School, Ribbleton

Bonie Tia

Tia is so sweet
She doesn't go *tweet-tweet*
She goes *miaow*
Not *bow-wow*
What animal is she?

Natasha Delany (10)
Ribbleton Avenue Methodist School, Ribbleton

Dontan's Funny Bunnies

I went on holiday and saw lots of bunnies,
It was so funny,
They popped up here, there and everywhere,
I think they play hide and seek.
It's funny to see rabbits on the beach,
We bought a torch, so we could see them at night,
Though they're cute.
When they popped out of their holes
It gave us a fright
Only because it was at night.

Danielle Howarth (10)
Ribbleton Avenue Methodist School, Ribbleton

My Molly Is Mad

She's lovely and funny
She cheers me up when I am sad.
She loves to fly around the room.
She has two friends, Austin and Kane who she likes to groom.
She loves to talk, she loves to dance,
She likes to eat bread,
She also likes to land on my dad's head.
Sometimes she's good
Sometimes she's bad
That's why my Molly is really mad.

Rebecca Lucia Thomas (10)
Ribbleton Avenue Methodist School, Ribbleton

The Night And The Wolf

It's a dark, dark night
The moon shines upon the land
There are shadows in the wood
One shadow reflects the beast of nightmares.
He slowly emerges out of the mist
He smells the air that belongs to him.
His eyes flash red, piercing the night
His hunger makes his jowl drool
As he smells the meal to come
And the fear he leaves behind
There is silence all around
As the beast approaches his prey
The fear created fills the air
The deer freezes on the spot
He makes his kill in one deadly pounce
With his belly full he slinks back into the night.

Josh Mealor (12)
Upton High School, Upton

I Have A . . .

I have a lively dog,
he runs around the park all day,
he's as pretty as a flower
blowing in the wind.
He's as happy as a clown,
but when the day has gone
he jumps on the end of my bed
and sleeps like a brick
that's my dog, Baggy.
I have a fluffy guinea pig
who munches on the grass all day long
they are soft and friendly
he likes a tickle under his chin and a brush
when I put them away he waits for his chocolate drop
and goes to sleep,
that's my guinea pigs, Smudge and Fudge.

Zoe Goulding (12)
Upton High School, Upton

I Love Little Pussy

I love little pussy, her coat is so warm
And if I don't hurt her she'll do me no harm
I'll show her respect
That's what she expects

So I'll defend her
So no one can end her
And I'll keep her calm
And stroke her with the end of my palm.

Matthew Hill (12)
Upton High School, Upton

Bush Dogs

They squeal until they get a meal
they walk and run
like they're having loads of fun
they're soft and brown
and never frown
they're fuzzy and cuddly
and you can never tell if they are muddy.

Jack Thornton (12)
Upton High School, Upton

Untitled

As soon as night comes
My cat stalks her prey as quiet as a mouse
She takes bigger and bigger strides to catch her prey
She leaps like a squirrel going to another tree
She finally catches it like a lion

As the sun rises she goes to sleep
She lays as a tortoise
She stays till the night comes again.

Holly Taylor (13)
Upton High School, Upton

The Elephant

The elephant strolls like an old man.
He stretches his trunk as long as a tree.
He flaps his huge ears in front of the herd
Getting ready to charge.
There he goes,
Defending his young ones from the intruder.
He sprints as fast as a cougar.
The intruder runs and runs till he's safe.
The intruder will never ever come back.

Ryan Wardle (12)
Upton High School, Upton

The Monkey

Monkey's swing, swing, swing
You see them bring, bring, bring
Delicious things, things, things
Like cola and rings, rings, rings
There are no more things, things, things
To see them bring, bring, bring
That's the end of the swing, swing, swing
No more words to sing, sing, sing.

Spencer Rogers (13)
Upton High School, Upton

The Sea Horse

Bright colours flash past,
Neon pink and yellow,
They travel together,
Defending themselves
Against the dark of the deep water,
Their eyes dart from left to right with caution,
Nobody can take their language away,
So unique, yet, secret.
This creature is called . . .

The sea horse.

Mary Freeman (12)
Upton High School, Upton

The Lion - King Of The Jungle

Mane waving free like a field of corn,
Teeth as white as a pile of snow on a winter morn.
King of the jungle from January to December,
With a roar like a firework on the 5th November.
Eyes clear like a tropical sea,
Roaming the wild for eternity.

Kia Cowley (12)
Upton High School, Upton

Cats Sleep Everywhere

Cats sleep everywhere
In the arm of the chair
On your lap
In your cap
In your dressing gown
On the church bell in town
On the end of your bed
After when they've been fed
Cats sleep everywhere
Cats sleep everywhere
But they don't care.
They prowl and purr
When you stroke their fur
And when they go to sleep
As quiet as a mouse,
Don't let out a peep
Cats sleep everywhere
Cats sleep everywhere.

Eve Matthews (12)
Upton High School, Upton

My Wicked Westie!

Small and nimble
Smooth as a spy
Jet the cats' mate
As playful as a baby
As proud as a prince
As hardy as a hobo
As speedy as a cheetah
As brave as a knight
As white as crisp, fresh snow
As hairy as Spartacus
A bone annihilator
His name is Tom Pan
And he is the best!

Matthew Haughton (13)
Upton High School, Upton

The Lion's Cave

The lion lay down in the dark gloomy cave
He stretched his paws out as far as he could
His baby cubs lay next to him
As close as a snail is to its shell.

The slow breeze made his mane wave side to side
The sound of monkeys and parrots echoed around the cave
He was almost invisible to the naked eye
So still, so lifeless you would think he was dead.

He slowly lifted his head and stood up
He walked to the entrance of the cave smoothly
Then jumped and landed on a zebra, breaking its back
He bit it by the neck and dragged it up to the cave.

The little cubs awoke and darted over to the meat
And started ripping into it like a chainsaw cutting into a tree.

After, they lay back down as the sun set
And the shimmering moon appeared in the night sky.

Patrick C Ryalls (12)
Upton High School, Upton

My Pets

Out in the garden hopping free
soft as a cloud, cuddly and loving
she is a Polish albino
as true as you get
running round lively
making a good pet
she is as soft and cuddly
as a teddy bear
as sleepy as a sloth
as playful as a pup
she is a Cavalier King Charles Spaniel
running round free
she likes a good walk
then she is as happy as Larry
when the sun goes down she receives her dressing gown
she is blind and deaf, but she still makes the perfect pet.

Heather Paton (13)
Upton High School, Upton

Tiger

The tiger hides in the long grass
Camouflaging his stripy skin,
He peeks through the grass watching,
He sits and waits a long time
With his fluffy fur flowing in the breeze
Like a fluffy blanket
Soon his prey will come and he will fight for food
So that he can survive.

Shannon Hunt (12)
Upton High School, Upton

Pig

Keep them alive and away from the chop,
Or their ears may just flop!
If you eat another sausage
I will call the cops,
They're pink and fat and go *oink*
If they fall on the floor they go *boink*
They live in a farm with some straw
And they eat the food from the floor.

Molly Cain (12)
Upton High School, Upton

Snow Leopard

The snow leopard hunts its prey
by waiting in the crispy snow
camouflaged like a hunter
striking his enemy

Running faster than the speed of light
scratching rocks as it passes
making sparks as a new car being made.

Benjamin Cardiff (12)
Upton High School, Upton

Little Fishy

The blue, little fish went swimming one day
Through the seaweed and avoiding the sharks
Then one day the scaly, slippery fish got eaten
By a big, fat, scary shark.

Marisa Salvi (12)
Upton High School, Upton

The Cat

The cat's eyes glow in the dark
as he sees the enemy approach.
It leaps off the bed like there's
someone after him.

The cat lands on the rough furry carpet,
as he gets closer to the door.
It is so dark, like he is locked in prison.
He moves around the quiet room
as he is trying to rob something.

He runs around the room
as he is playing with a piece of string.
He licks his fur, he is giving himself a bath.

Rafeea Islam (12)
Upton High School, Upton

A Dolphin

A dolphin will always be a dolphin
A dolphin swims along the cold sea waters
Silently floating along a big wave.
Side to side with their small daughters.
Jumping in the air its shiny skin glistens,
Desperately trying to find some tasty fish
A calming peaceful sound you hear if you listen
Yummy, yum he chomps on a tasty dish.
Dolphins and humans mix like chocolate and a cookie,
If we help them they might be lucky.
We don't want these creatures to fade away
So help us save dolphins today.

India Cotgreave (12)
Upton High School, Upton

Turtle

It swam by me like a bird in the sea
Slick like a seal.
Fishes swim by it like a friend.
Its hard smooth shell
Protected it from most predators
Its flippers made it glide through the sea.
Its green and black camouflage made it hard to see.
This is a turtle.

Neirin McDonald (12)
Upton High School, Upton

The Wolf

His fur was so soft and shiny,
He looked like a little baby.
His eyes were glittering,
He looked like he was crying.
He was moving slowly,
Then jumping on something suddenly.
Why would the wolf be jumping?
I couldn't see anything.
Shaking, he shook his head.
He has broken his leg.
He dragged himself across the forest.
His blood was as warm as the sun.
As it was flowing out like flood,
I felt the need to run.
Kneeling down, I saw a scary man.
A gun, that's what he was holding.
I felt the wolf had stopped breathing.
He hasn't broken his leg,
He was dead!

Karin Madericova (11)
Wood Green High School, Wednesbury

Dancing Dolphins

Dolphins are so cute
They really are so much fun
Dancing in the sun.

Sophia Elton (11)
Wood Green High School, Wednesbury

Cat Poem

Cats, cats, don't like rats.
Cats, cats, don't like bats.
Cats, cats, don't like hats
And so don't I.

Cats, cats, don't like dogs
Cats, cats, don't like boats
Cats, cats, don't like soaps
And so don't I.

Cats, cats, don't like baths
Cats, cats, don't like tasks
Cats, cats, don't like masks
And so don't I.

Chloe Bennett (11)
Wood Green High School, Wednesbury

Dino Dinosaur Poem!

He was named Dino Dinosaur
He liked to be a pain in the neck
He was a Blue Peter dinosaur
With a button on his eye
And yoghurt carton thighs.

His teeth were made out of plastic
And his claws were made out of cards
His tail waved side to side
But he could not roar or walk
Nowadays they are made out of flesh and blood.

Davina Sanoi (11)
Wood Green High School, Wednesbury

Pat, Cat And Rat!

Cat the rat he is fat
And black and white
He likes Rat the cat
Rat the cat hates
Cat the rat because
Cat the rat ate
Rat's family so

Cat ate Rat so Pat the
Bat hit Cat.
Cat likes bats that are wood.
Then Cat spits
Rat out then
Pat the bat gets
Cat the rat a
Rat a cat hat
Gets Pat in the hat
A bat hat.

Matthew Gardner (11)
Wood Green High School, Wednesbury

My Cat!

My cat got bitten by a rat,
He sleeps on the front door mat.
He loves to play in the fog,
Then he got caught by a mean dog.

Now he slithers like a snake,
Because he got bitten by a rat,
And got caught by a dog,
Who looks like a big mean rug.

Now my cat has only three legs,
I feel sorry for my cat called Jug.

Emily Rowton (11)
Wood Green High School, Wednesbury

Polar Bears

Polar bears are as white as snow
Polar bears don't fright
Polar bears are cuddly
Polar bears are snuggly
Polar bears love snow
Polar bears know
Polar bears love sun
Polar bears love to run
Polar bears are old
Polar bears are sold
Polar bears are funny
Polar bears make money
Polar bears are crying
Polar bears are dying.

Alice Legister (11)
Wood Green High School, Wednesbury

Adopt A Tiger

There, a tiger going for a snooze,
Then the afternoon comes,
Until I see,
A nasty sight,
Sparks, flames and smoke,
The terrified tiger,
Runs for her life,
Against the battle of fire,
Ready for her day,
Waiting to come,
Adopt her now!

Brandon Rhys Moseley (12)
Wood Green High School, Wednesbury

Polar Bears Poem

Polar bears, polar bears
silky and smooth
polar bears, polar bears
like to move
They're furry and white
and so tight
they always fight like a knight!
They're caring and kind but you will find
polar bears, polar bears
need help, if you want one
give us a shout!
They love meat and treats
surely you adopted one
they're just too sweet!

Courtney Nock (11)
Wood Green High School, Wednesbury

Hamster

Hamster, hamster, sleeps all day and wakes up at night.
Hamster cheeks grow very big when they put food in their mouth.
Their whiskers are very tickly when they jump on you.
Their cage gets very messy when they put everything in their bed.
Hamsters get all their food into their bed
Then we give them more food.

Kieran Caville (11)
Wood Green High School, Wednesbury

The Anaconda

As the yellow snake slithers through the grass,
it approaches the deer
suddenly wraps around the deer
as it starts swallowing it whole
as it eats it all, the snake has to go

After the deer was gone
that the snake swallowed in one
it slithered and hissed up the tree
then wrapped itself around the tree
then the animals all peek.

Matthew Jones (11)
Wood Green High School, Wednesbury

My Dog, Mog

My pet Mog is really a dog,
he's faster than a dog,
but slower than a log,
he can't be a dog,
because his snout's like a hog.

He looks out the window,
all day long,
but really likes to
run and pong.

He likes to have a good old fuss,
but hates when people stop the fuss,
he likes to play with Gus,
but hates when he jumps on the bus.

He loves playing football,
but hates watching it,
so go back out and play it,
now go back in and watch it,
because you might have a really good treat.

Luke Simpson-Shaw (11)
Wood Green High School, Wednesbury

A Puppy Called Huppy

My puppy is called Huppy and is very cute, he is a Beagle.
I went to the shop to get a puppy.
When I got it, I hopped it and went to another place with dogs.
I finally found my dog which I named Huppy,
and she was active, caring and was the perfect dog for me.
When I got home I moaned,
because it was night and I needed to sleep
so I couldn't play with my dog called Huppy.
In the morning I went downstairs and she was not there.
I cried and cried like an enormous waterfall,
but then I heard something outside in the garden
and so I looked . . . It was Huppy.
I found my fearless dog.
I was so happy I could even jump off a mountain.
That was the best day of my life.

Preeya Sharma (11)
Wood Green High School, Wednesbury

Wolf! Wolf!

A wolf is an endangered species
They are dangerous if they are let off their leashes
They're agile at hunting but calm when it ceases
They are as fast as a bird and as cunning as a fox
At full moon they sit and howl!
But when day breaks they look and prowl
And they are really hairy just like a towel.

Ryan Jones (11)
Wood Green High School, Wednesbury

Tiger Poem

Tigers are quick, they are there in a flick.
They are as quick as lightning in a flash.
Their black and orange fur sways left and right in the wind.
When they are hungry they chase and chase.
Eventually they jump, hit and pound viciously on their prey
like they were a punching bag.
After that they just relax whilst roaring and yawning.

Nathan Patel (11)
Wood Green High School, Wednesbury

My kitten

My kitten is very sweet,
but it hits me when I eat,
so I give it a little kick,
then it starts to lick!

It likes playing with my teddy,
and my brother named it Weddy,
it always sits on my map
wearing my bright red hat!

Zaynah Fiaz (11)
Wood Green High School, Wednesbury

My Crazy Cat

My crazy cat does the craziest things.
She talks about her crazy life after she escaped from the pet shop.
She said when she was in the jungle
She fought with a tiger and an alligator!
My crazy cat!
She told me about her trip to China
and her karate class with world-famous Jackie Chan.
My crazy cat!
My cat said she sang in a concert with Cheryl Cole!
My crazy cat!
I wonder what other adventures she will have . . . ?

My crazy cat!

Aiesha Kauser (11)
Wood Green High School, Wednesbury

Koala Bears Are My Favourite Animals

K oala bears
O versized noses
A re my favourite animal
L ovely
A nd so cute.

B eautiful
E ucalyptus
A mazing
R esters
S leep sweetly.

Abby Wilde (11)
Wood Green High School, Wednesbury

The Lion

Keeping camouflage the thing is crawling,
There is something in sight,
What could it be?
He is the king of the jungle!
His mane is hairy,
His tail swishes side to side like a snake's body,
Positioning himself ready to pounce . . .
Rrrrrrrr!
Landing on the deer the lion chomps away
While the African sun is burning down on the lion.

Liam Busher (11)
Wood Green High School, Wednesbury

Who Am I?

I live in a county as frozen as your freezer (and more).
People say we are great swimmers and we look like saucers.
I have wings as wide as a football pitch.
I can't see my legs because I'm as fast as the world.
My colours are negative and positive.
I have a scaly scrumptious lovely diet that I might share with my family.
Who am I?

A: Penguin.

Chinedum Mj Nmerukini (11)
Wood Green High School, Wednesbury

Dolphin

The acrobatic animal slowly entered the pool,
Elegantly it swam to a stool.
As it swam under all you could see was its bottle nose.
Suddenly the creature dove into the air
Then entered its lair . . .

Caitlin Davies (11)
Wood Green High School, Wednesbury

Jasper

J asper is cute and fluffy
A t home he is always sleeping
S wimming in his grandad's pond
P ulling on his lead to go on to the field
E ating all his brother's food
R unning round the garden.

Ashley Cross (11)
Wood Green High School, Wednesbury

Guessing Game

Disobedient, like a child
Wild and unpredictable
Devilish, daring, deficient
As they make their way across the African land.

Hunting for food
They daren't attract attention
Because if it goes wrong
The outcome is dismay.

Brave and courageous
Valiant and adventurous
A fussy eater, only the best will do
Like zebra, rhino and hippo.

What animal do you think it is?

Millie Boulton (11)
Wood Green High School, Wednesbury

The Cat!

All you can hear is breaking twigs
Then it comes with a swagger in its step.
Its long tail comes right up to your knees.
It has a very cute sneeze.
Its long slim body wraps round your legs.
The cheekiness in it draws it to jump on your lap
Just missing your bacon-filled bap!
You push this black and white animal, brushing it off your legs.
Its noisy cry is so cute.
It's kind, friendly and can be timid
That when I go to stroke him, he pounds back into the bushes.

Eve Wilson (11)
Wood Green High School, Wednesbury

Kittens

K is for kind
I is for imagination
T is for talent
T is for tiredness
E is for elegant
N is for nice
S is for sweet

But we love them in every single way.

Lily Bradley (11)
Wood Green High School, Wednesbury

Tigers

A tiger is
Really fast
And in a race
It's never last.

They climb a tree
To see what's there
But in the end
It's only a pear.

You can call a tiger
A huge cat
Although its prey will say
It's a killer rat.

The Arctic tiger
Is as ferocious as a bear
But in the wild
They're really rare.

Tiger can swim
Just like me
But unlike me
They can't catch a bee.

Danyaal Saeed (11)
Wood Green High School, Wednesbury

I Have A Cat

I have a cat
Who sits on the mat
She's a bit like Tom, you know from Tom and Jerry
Always strange but very, very merry.

I have a cat
Her name is Pat.
By day she's a sleeping sloth,
By night she's a flying moth.

My cat, sweet, sweet Pat
Like Tom and Jerry, very merry.
A sleeping sloth very lazy
But I love my cat . . . Pat!

Ethan Nwokeforo (12)
Wood Green High School, Wednesbury

Cheetahs

C heetahs running through the jungle with their big paws
H appily catching animals with their big claws
E ating and shredding meat with their big teeth
E asily hiding away inside the jungle leaf
T earing and eating all this food does not make them fat
A nimals like this big are related to a cat!
H elplessly getting caught by poachers
S adly there are not that many left!

Courtney June Handley (12)
Wood Green High School, Wednesbury

About A Kitten

K ittens are cute
I n a world they live
T hey always seem to stink
T hey always seem to annoy
E ngraved in their hearts love you
N ever will you ever forget them
S o you know they are always there.

Danny Horobin (11)
Wood Green High School, Wednesbury

Boxer Dogs

Boxer dogs are loud
And are as soft as a cloud.
Sometimes dumb,
Sometimes funny.
They sometimes come
And cost a lot of money.

As big as a clam
And as bouncy as a lamb.
Sometimes fun,
Sometimes dozy,
They rarely come
And are really nosy!

Grace Guest (11)
Wood Green High School, Wednesbury

Kittens

Kittens that are kind
Have a lively mind
Inspired with many ideas.
They perform the most talented tricks
For just a cute little kitten.
So ticklish yet so cuddly,
She just can't let go of me!
As enthusiastic as can be
However, she is naughty!
But kittens are worth your life
Don't you agree?

Sharmila Begum (11)
Wood Green High School, Wednesbury

My Animal Poem

Slippery scales, big tails
The biggest ones are always females.
In most lakes
There's fish of all kinds of makes!
They usually take rods
For the specific reasons, you can leave them on pods.

Thomas Bradbury (11)
Wood Green High School, Wednesbury

Cats, Cats, Cats

Cats, cats, cats
Sleek and shy
As they creep around.
Cats looking at the rats
And their slithery tails.
Cats prowling and looking for food
Oh he's got something!
Is it a bird, is it a mouse?
Cats in the moonlight
Looking for a friend.

As they come in in the morning
They jump on your bed for attention
Then it's food time, what will he have?
He's off again on the hunt
It's another day.
He's gone to the bay
And seen Ray!

Katie Frampton (11)
Wood Green High School, Wednesbury

Wolves

Wolves are fast, wolves are nimble,
They're in packs not with stacks.
Although they're small, they can hunt a mammal standing tall.
Wolves can smell if prey is near, either a rabbit or a deer.
When they run it's not for fun, they're on a hunt.
When it's winter they go to bed,
All trees are now dying or dead.
Spring is here, the wolves awake
This is another challenge they must take.
But now it's time to go after all.
The wolves are not for show.
We should not harm them in any way
If we do it will be the end of their day.

Joseph Peake (11)
Wood Green High School, Wednesbury

My Puppy

I have a puppy named Dottie,
She has a sister named Lottie.
Together they're cute and fluffy
And their mom's name is Muffy.

Let's talk all about Dottie
She is cute, loyal but potty
All day long she rolls in a puddle
And then comes in for a great big cuddle.

Next comes Lottie,
I think she's calmer than her sister Dottie.
Lottie is fun
And her favourite food is a bun.

Niamh Lloyd (11)
Wood Green High School, Wednesbury

A Poem About Monkeys

Monkeys are cute
Oh so cool
Naughty
Killer climbers
Educational
You should all love monkeys.

Brandon Spruce (11)
Wood Green High School, Wednesbury

Jaguars

J olting as fast as they can go
A lways fighting over meat
G rabbing all they can get
U rgently attacking their prey
A ngrily fighting each other because the other got the meat
R ocking riot round the rainforest.

Joseph Bull (11)
Wood Green High School, Wednesbury

My Best Animal - Spanish Bull

S o silly
P roblems caused
A re admired
N aughty
I s imaginable
S peedy
H armful

B easts
U nbearable pain caused by them
L oved by some people
L aziness is not found in them.

Yasmeen Javid Salloo (11)
Wood Green High School, Wednesbury

Alligator Snapping Turtle

It swims day and night eating fish.
It only has to see you then
It hunts!
Once that 30cm jaw shuts
You're finished with!

James Rutter-Corbett (11)
Wood Green High School, Wednesbury

Sharks

S harks
H ave amazing talent
A re the best
R ipping teeth
K iller of fish
S have fish in half with their teeth.

Arjun Sehmbi (11)
Wood Green High School, Wednesbury

Jingo, The Crazy Poochy Dog

J iggy, like a meerkat dog
I rresponsible, always doing naughties on the carpet
N aughty, he tricks Trouble, my kitten
G runt, he grunts like a pig
O verjoyed, he is full of fun and energy.

Amber Gee (11)
Wood Green High School, Wednesbury

Tigers

T iger stripes are fascinating so they know who's who
I ntelligent tigers solving puzzles to earn treats
G aming around, running, following others
E ating away on their scrumptious meat
R eal life, they can fight for different reasons
S wimming is most tigers' favourite thing

I am a tiger.

Bethany Alicia Hyde (11)
Wood Green High School, Wednesbury

Little Rabbit

Little rabbit you are so cute
You may be small but not like a newt.

You hop up and down and all around
Plus you do it without a sound.

You always nibble on a green leaf
While it nibbles on a piece of corned beef.

You always play
Until I say, 'Nay!'
Too bad you went
Because for you I have sent
Oh little rabbit so small.

Tyler James Patrick Branigan (11)
Wood Green High School, Wednesbury

Rabbit Poem

R abbits are as fluffy as cotton wool
A pples and carrots are their delight
B right eyes and bushy tails
B ouncing up to greet you each time
I deal pets for children
T witching noses as they play.

Laura Brown (11)
Wood Green High School, Wednesbury

My Animal Poem

I move gracefully in the tall trees.
I have legs like sticks or stilts.
I have a neck like a large log.
I have pointy ears to hear pesky predators.
I have a swishy tail to flick biting bugs.
I have hooves like babies clapping.
I live in the dusty plains of Africa.
I am a . . . ?

A: Giraffe.

Kara Mason (11)
Wood Green High School, Wednesbury

I Hate Spiders!

Why do I hate spiders?
Well, here it goes.
They're creepy, they're crawly, they're scary and did I mention
They're creepy, crawly and scary!

With their big round body
And eight skinny legs
They tiptoe all around your house
And . . .
Up your back!

Winter's now here
There's a dozen in your house
They're looking for somewhere
Just warm and sound
By the time coldness has vanished
And warmth is back.
My house is covered
With a huge blanket of white
And I guarantee you
It's not snow!

Abida Khanom (11)
Wood Green High School, Wednesbury

My Awesome Animal

As fierce as the Roman army but as quiet as a mouse.
My dog lies in wait ready to pounce.
She leaps in the air like a frog or a flea.
She lands in her bowl whilst spilling her tea.

Joe Devey (11)
Wood Green High School, Wednesbury

The Parrot

Ungraceful he seems,
When he flies through the wind
He is like a gushhawk
With an ear-piercing squawk.
He flies away at the slightest dismay.
Loud at night.
He will put up a fight
If you try to tame the parrot.

Connor Mason (11)
Wood Green High School, Wednesbury

My Fast Cheetah

My cheetah is very fast and cheeky.
My cheetah can hide in the deep smooth grass.
My cheetah is faster than a race horse.
My cheetah looks after his family.
My cheetah is all he can be.
My cheetah is adorable.
My cheetah loves all of me.
My cheetah loves and cares for me.
My cheetah likes to stare at me.

Wesley Dylan Ebanks (11)
Wood Green High School, Wednesbury

My Cat

My cat was bitten by a kitten.
He likes licking and kicking
But he doesn't care if he tears the walls apart.
The cat likes food but he makes a mess!
When I have Nescafé coffee
He knocks it out my hand and licks it off the floor.
He is naughty like a devil!
That's my cat for you.

Harry Garrison (11)
Wood Green High School, Wednesbury

Kitten Poem

My kitten has been bitten by an even older kitten.
I feel sorry for the poor lad really and truly I do.
He has a friend called Pat.
Pat loves to chat so does my cat.
But my cat loves to jump in my lap all the time.
My cat has a mat and he loves to have a nap.

Shanique Grant (11)
Wood Green High School, Wednesbury

My Dog

My dog is as fast as lightning
As she chases the wild rabbit through the long green grass.
Sleeping on the mat she lies there
Calmly sleeping into tomorrow's day.
She wakes up with a mischievous smile
Then yawns and goes to chase cats for a while.
I get the lead, she runs away, I chase
But she is like the wind impossible to catch.
I take her out for a walk
And she growls at the obvious cats walking by.
Whilst at the field she tries to catch the butterfly
Doing back flips to avoid her.
She sneaks up like a ninja and the butterfly is gone.

Jack Rees (11)
Wood Green High School, Wednesbury

All About The Jaguar

In the rainforest
There is a jaguar
That travels the lands
And goes so far.
Its fur is spotty
And golden like the sand.
Its home, the forest land.

The jaguar can run like the wind
It sneaks on its prey throughout the day
From dusk till dawn it prowls throughout the trees
The branches hang low hiding the jaguar below.
Its teeth are like thunderbolts
Striking through the clouds.
The jaguar bites its frightened prey
Come what may.
The animal's dead,
Her family get fed.

Neil Boulton (11)
Wood Green High School, Wednesbury

Polar Bears

Polar bears are so cute that they make me want to puke.
Their fur is softer than a lovely nice warm blanket.
Their noses are like a big rock covered in snowflakes
Their claws are really bigger and sharper
Than the sharpest ever knife in the world.
Polar bears' smell senses are one hundred times better
Than a human being.
Their ears are much more solid than a big ball of ice.

Ibrahim Ahmed (11)
Wood Green High School, Wednesbury

Compare The Alexander

Mad, messy meerkat, Alexander to be exact.
He's cute and furry who dresses in a little red gown.
He goes to the Sahara looking up to his grandfather.
Best friends with a mentally ill scientist
Who lives in the geek computer world.
Alexander has petite, beady eyes, no, that's not a lie.
I bet you know that Compare The Market is the most brilliant site, *ever!*
Simples!

Shannon Louise Woodbine (11)
Wood Green High School, Wednesbury

Animal Mystery Extraordinaire

This is an animal who lives high up in the mountains,
Who builds a nest on the cliff edges.
Its speed is extraordinary, it's as fast as a lightning bolt.
For its prey it gobbles diminutive mice and some smaller birds.
Its feathers are as smooth as a peach.
It's as peaceful as silence as it creeps up on its unsuspecting prey.
You couldn't see it coming; it's as quick as a flash.
Its cry is as loud as a lion's roar.
Its claws are as sharp as a samurai's blade
As it catches and pierces its prey.
Its amber eyes are as bright as the blinding sun
As its stare pierces you like a dagger.
It soars high into the sky,
Just waiting to dive down and make its catch!
If you've read this poem thoroughly
You might've figured it out by now
That the mystery animal behind this story is the falcon!
So now you know!

Sasha Britton (11)
Wood Green High School, Wednesbury

Arachnophobia

These creatures are everywhere,
How can we bear?
They crawl in the stillness
Throughout our home.
The alien in an army
Waiting to strike!
Hairy, scary, that's what they are.
Halting at a dead stop they wait.
Some of us hate them, some of us love them
I adore them, my friend can't bear them.
He fears their fangs; he's scared they'll bite.
If he gets bitten, if he does, he'll definitely get a fright!

Gurwinder Singh (11)
Wood Green High School, Wednesbury

Young Writers Information

We hope you have enjoyed reading this book - and that you will continue to enjoy it in the coming years.

If you like reading and writing poetry drop us a line, or give us a call, and we'll send you a free information pack.

Alternatively if you would like to order further copies of this book or any of our other titles, then please give us a call or log onto our website at **www.youngwriters.co.uk**

Young Writers Information
Remus House
Coltsfoot Drive
Peterborough
PE2 9BF
(01733) 890066